The Church in the Next Decade

The Church
in the Next Decade

BY EUGENE CARSON BLAKE

THE MACMILLAN COMPANY, NEW YORK
COLLIER-MACMILLAN LTD., LONDON

Library of Congress Catalog Card Number: 66-25501

FIRST PRINTING

The Macmillan Company, New York
Collier-Macmillan Canada Ltd., Toronto, Ontario

Printed in the United States of America

Grateful acknowledgment is made for permission to reprint the following:

To Presbyterian Life, Inc., for "The Meaning of the Reformation" originally published in the October 27, 1951, issue of *Presbyterian Life* under the title of "Freedom and Authority in Church and State."

To The Christian Century Foundation for "Law and Order and Christian Duty" reprinted from the November 1963 issue of *The Pulpit*, and for "Afrikaners' Five Blind Spots" reprinted from the February 10, 1960, issue of *The Christian Century*.

To The Methodist Publishing House for "Should Church Property Be Taxed?" as it appeared in the April 1962 issue of *Together Magazine*.

To The Lawrenceville School for "That Controversial Ecumenical Movement, 1965" which originally appeared in the Summer 1965 issue of *Lawrentian* published by The Lawrenceville School, Lawrenceville, New Jersey.

To the Princeton Theological Seminary for "Prophet and Priest, but Not King" which originally appeared in the October 1962 issue of *The Princeton Seminary Bulletin*.

To Fordham University Press for "Some Implications of a United Church" which originally appeared in the Spring 1966 issue of *Thought* under the title "A United Church: Evangelical, Catholic and Reformed."

1369049

CONTENTS

PREFACE

THIS volume contains a collection of essays, articles, and sermons on some subjects that I regard as important for the life of the Christian churches during the coming decade. They are offered in the hope that the experience and reflection of one churchman may stimulate additional reflection and discussion by others.

The scheme of the volume is simple. The introductory section, "The Church and the Reformation Faith," contains four essays outlining my understanding of the Christian faith and the task of the Church. The second section, "Contemporary Pressures," takes up problems such as race, poverty, and peace that represent challenges to all Christians today and will continue to be the concerns of any religious group that hopes to make its insights felt in the world during the coming decade. It should be noted that some of these articles were written in specific historical situations—though I would hope that their significance extends beyond the circumstances of their creation. In the final section, "The New Ecumenical Reformation," I try to explore some directions in which the Church is moving in this ecumenical age and to offer some suggestions as to how best to approach the problems and challenges of this age.

It will be clear from the very beginning that I speak as an American and as a Presbyterian in the Reformed tradition. I have no illusions that my own particular heritage has a monopoly on Christian truth, but I feel that the Ecumenical Movement is best served when it is regarded, not as a quest for the lowest common denominator upon which Christians can cooperate, but rather as the interaction of loyal representatives of distinct traditions under the guidance of the Holy Spirit. I thus hope that this collection will be useful as a contribution to ecumenical dialogue by one Christian who feels that his own tradition has much to contribute and much to learn from other Christians.

The Church
and the
Reformation Faith

Chapter 1

THE MEANING OF THE
REFORMATION *

THE history of the past four hundred years in Europe and the West has been the history of an attempt to replace with something else the cultural, political, and theological unity of the Middle Ages. We are told by historians that the thirteenth century in Europe was a great era because art, learning, religion, and the common life of man all then reached climaxes of creative unity. Although it is true that our best historians today question the sweeping romantic generalizations of the past about this creative, corporate unity of the Middle Ages, still it is a pretty picture that is painted of life in Europe before the modern Protestant era had begun.

We see the peasant at his plow cultivating fertile fields under the protecting shadow of his liege lord's castle walls. We watch him kneeling before the altar of a stately parish church—a church that he and his fellows have built with their own hands in simple Gothic beauty for their love of God. Solemn music fills the fragrant, holy air as the sun shines through stained glass that we still try our best to copy.

We see universities where the faculties of theology and science are one—speaking the same language—creatively preparing the way for the *Summa* of Saint Thomas, the greatest book of theology and philosophy ever written—so the story goes. We see villages and small cities—with an almost nostalgic longing we see them— true communities in the basic sense that all their members know each other and feel that they belong to one another. The baron in his castle knows his place and its responsibilities as does the

---

* The following address was given at the First Presbyterian Church, Philadelphia, on October 23, 1951, when Dr. Blake was installed as Stated Clerk of the Presbyterian Church in the U.S.A.

3

serf upon his land, and neither would dream of changing places with the other. A mosaic of liege relationships binds all together, and at the pinnacle is the Bishop of Rome, before whom even kings and emperors bow.

It is a pretty picture that loses nothing in the telling, especially when it is contrasted with the ugly picture of our world today.

For today we see a Western world in which men are worried, restless, and nostalgic everywhere. The farmer's son flees the tractor's seat the first chance he gets, to go off to the freedom of the big and dirty city where he becomes one of a crowd of lonely factory hands hired and fired at the dictates of a relentless economic cycle. If in need he is cared for not by family or neighbors but by an impersonal welfare commission which, if it is generous, takes away his self-reliance and which, if it is harsh, turns him into a bitter enemy of society.

Typically, he doesn't go to church—not even to the ugly Akron-style auditorium where jazzy hymns are sung to the accompaniment of a squeaky organ and where the sun, if it shines through the city's smoke, shines through windows too long uncleaned. He lives in less space, closer to other human beings, than man has ever had to live before, but knows and is known by fewer of them than any village boy. He has no relationships that he can count upon. Families break up with divorce for the slightest kinds of reasons. His boss and supervisors are enemies and his union is dominated by big shots who scarcely seem to remember that he exists.

Nearby his slum home rise the stately pseudo-Gothic buildings of the university, but the professors there are no longer a faculty who can discuss together the great questions of humanity in the light of their several disciplines. They don't know one another's language. Psychologists and philosophers scoff at each other's subject matter and techniques while both together look down their scholastic noses at the theologians. Yet in their turn they are despised by the natural scientists who, however, find their fame and prestige not dependent, as they would wish, on their advancement of knowledge, but upon the utility of their discoveries to the new aristocracy of engineers.

The Church—no, we cannot longer say the Church—the churches are divided and competing and often isolated from the main stream of life and culture. Art and architecture reach new lows each decade. Poetry delights itself in obscurity, and the nations, hamstrung by vice and greed, vie with each other in war and peace—none knowing any authority higher than competing self-interest, more or less enlightened.

So modern man, who won his freedom and prosperity at great effort, finds his victory empty and his success a burden. His frustrated and troubled mind cracks under the strain of his fears and loneliness, palliated by an ever faster tempo of life and ever lower forms of recreation. Finally, when the pressure becomes too great, he becomes an unstable fanatic—whether political, mental, or religious.

This is the picture that is painted of our modern world as contrasted with high moments of the Middle Ages. I need hardly say that these pictures and this contrast are neither altogether true nor altogether false. Historians now admit that the unity, beauty, and order of the Middle Ages was not as ideal as our nostalgia sometimes pictures it. Further, it must be admitted that there were many forces which were in process of destroying that unity long before the Reformers wrested the northern half of Europe away from the political and theological control of the Pope and the Roman Catholic Church. For example, we may cite Franciscan piety, Gothic naturalism in Chaucer and Boccaccio, the worldwide adventures of crusader and businessman, the revival of classic learning, the successful intellectual battle of the philosophic nominalists, the beginnings of free enterprise—all these quite apart from the Reformation had their parts in breaking up the medieval synthesis.

Among Presbyterians, I need not hesitate to use the word *sin* to indicate the basic reason for the Church's loss of its spiritual and moral leadership of Europe. The system of feudalism allied with natural greed led men to think of bishoprics and monasteries as nothing but sources of wealth, and it became not unusual for boys to be elected bishops to keep the income in the family. Simony, all kinds of corruption, overlaid the Church from top to bottom, from pope to priest. Superstition became the handmaiden of greed as salvation was bought and sold, and the Church, for its selfish interests, made available or withheld the sacraments. And to make the medieval picture correspond a little more closely to reality, we need remember that it should show the poverty, squalor, inhumanity, ignorance, and injustice that did in fact exist.

Attempts were made to reform both the Church and all medieval life long before the Reformation. Saint Francis and Saint Dominic were both partially successful in that their movements proved that Christ still lived and loved and saved. But the popes successfully resisted all challenges to their authority when the conciliar movements were defeated. Yet the unrest remained, and unenlightened ecclesiastical totalitarianism was doomed. Men were no longer satisfied with things as they were, and, with or without a Protestant Reformation, Europe and the West were going to be very different in the modern day. The Protestant Reformation can properly be thought of in one respect not so much as revolt against the beliefs, practices, and authority of the Roman Church in the name of religious freedom as an attempt, not yet completed, to substitute a new kind of order and authority for that which was in any case doomed to go.

More briefly, I want to correct some of the outlines of the modern picture, too. No picture of modern life is properly realistic which omits appreciation of the values of freedom and release won by the successive liberal revolutions. Free enterprise has not only lifted the standard of living but has given spiritual gifts, too, offering every man a chance to stand erect and carve his own future by his own efforts. Schools for everyone, increase of knowledge (especially scientific), increase of philanthropy, technological advance—all these are so well known that I need not dwell upon them. But it is also true that despite all the advances of these last four hundred years modern man is generally frustrated and fearful (not without reason), and few would claim that television, chrome cars, aluminum tube chairs, comic books, movies, or even organized baseball, which I love, are sufficient marks of a great culture or civilization.

The Protestant Reformation was the attempt of some Christians to find once more in the gospel of Jesus Christ the insights and values which would redeem the Church and leaven the new and free society. In all its branches Protestantism established the necessary ground for, and gave new insights into, the liberty of the Christian man. It was and is a faith of freedom. But how to keep freedom from degenerating into anarchy? If the old unity was broken, how to create a new society, a new corporate sense of community? This was the problem that faced the great Reformers, and there is little disagreement among historians to the proposition that it was John Calvin who, more effectively than any other, grappled with the problem of freedom and authority in Church and State. He it was who produced the principles of its solution, that even today is the only alternative to a totalitarianism of the right or the left.

Although I would be careful not to be misunderstood as supposing that the tradition of which our Church is the inheritor is the perfect and only fully Christian tradition (my conviction is far from that), I do think it is fitting to remind you of some of the contributions of Calvinism to the continuing reformation of both Church and State. For it is my conviction that it is as possible for us to be too modest about our Church and faith as it is to be overweeningly and pharisaically proud of them.

There are two specific emphases of Calvin and the Calvinistic tradition which we have inherited that seem to me particularly pertinent.

Central and first is the emphasis on the sovereignty of God. Quite apart from any other reasons for its acceptance, a recognition of the mighty rule of God becomes a vital necessity if human freedom is not to degenerate into anarchy. Revolutions are never very pretty things. I suggest to you that the major reason that our American Revolution was not attended by the type of terror and purge that most revolutions bring in their wake was the pervasive influence of a faith in a sovereign God among its leaders. When these bold men reluctantly decided to make a declaration of independence from the authority of the British crown, they did it, both Calvinist and deist, with a lively sense of their continued obligation to the greater King. Though written somewhat later, the last stanza of our national hymn expresses this fact in classic form:

> *Our fathers' God, to thee,*
> *Author of liberty,*
> *To thee we sing:*
> *Long may our land be bright*
> *With freedom's holy light;*
> *Protect us by thy might,*
> *Great God, our King.*

Criticism of freedom in favor of authority will always be persuasive unless men accept the faith that *Christian freedom is always freedom under God.* We have the essence of it in the familiar hymn:

> *Make me a captive, Lord,*
> *And then I shall be free.*

In the light of our heritage, you and I have a grave responsibility always to be sure that the freedom and individualism we espouse is not that humanistic license that has done so much to make the soul of modern man tired of what he thought was freedom and turn in his soul's sickness to tyranny old or new.

Under this first basic Calvinistic emphasis, and subsidiary to it, is a second principle: Authority in Church and State, as a practical matter, must never be in the hands of any single person but must always be lodged in a group of freely elected representatives of all. As illustration of what I mean, I hope you will pardon a personal reference. A number of my friends, including, I am sorry to say, a number of members of the Presbyterian Church, betrayed considerable ignorance about what a stated clerk is when they read the announcement of my election last spring. When it was explained that it was the highest permanent executive office in our Church, most then began severely to criticize the inadequacy of the title for an office apparently so important.

Now while I could wish, especially in relationship to other churches and to the state, that the title did carry with it more meaning and prestige than it does, nevertheless this old title does illustrate exactly this principle of Presbyterianism which I am now discussing. Authority and prestige are not given to individuals by Presbyterians. The office into which I have been installed is important only as it reflects the authority and prestige of the General Assembly whose servant the stated clerk is. And to make it sure and clear, there is elected a moderator who is given the prestige without much power. And to the man who inevitably has more ecclesiastical power than any other in the Church (due to the authority and size of the General Assembly and to the infrequency of its meetings), Presbyterians make sure he remembers his real place by naming him, not *bishop* or *chancellor* or *provost* or any prestige-bestowing title, but a *clerk,* even though the adjective *stated* is added to take away a little of the implication of his being but a scrivener.

This I suggest to you is illustrative of our basic Calvinistic tradition of how men should organize authority in their groupings, whether in Church or State. We should remember, however, that this Presbyterian technique of government is no more pure democracy than it is monarchy or tyranny. Our fathers in Britain were right, I believe, in resisting the independents as much as they did the authoritarians, even though England was lost to them in the process. In recent years it has been difficult for us sometimes to understand why our ancestors were so much against the Congregationalists. A recent court decision has belatedly made some Congregationalists wonder whether perhaps their polity was a little too democratic to enable Congregationalists legally to do anything together. Of course, the fact is that the independent spirit in the United States has been so powerful that most churches have tended to be congregational in fact, whatever their form of government.

I stand before you tonight, however, as one who believes that the best thing we Presbyterians can do for the world and for the Church today is to recapture for ourselves and make available to others the essential values of representative constitutional government. There have been too many Presbyterian Church members who have supposed that they were free to act as they pleased in the Church of which they are members. There are even elders who suppose that they are free to attack the program of the Church in public speech or print just as their individual idiosyncrasies lead them. They are shocked whenever a session proceeds even to threaten to discipline them—reminding them of their ordination vows. There are, alas, Presbyterian ministers who suppose that they are good Presbyterians when they freely flout the considered and prayerful actions of their presbyteries. Some of these are ignorant of what kind of Church it is to which they belong and whose form of government they have solemnly sworn that they approved. Others know better but refuse to believe in the possibility that they may be wrong, which, by Presbyterian definition, you are when you are in the minority against the considered and prayerful decision of your brethren. And those who, when they come up against this authority, claim the right to flout it in the name of conscience and the Holy Spirit would do well, as will the rest of us, to read through thoughtfully the first chapter of the Form of Government, which is an essential part of our Presbyterian Constitution. Let me quote for you several sentences from these preliminary principles, which I believe are the finest statements to be found anywhere of the Calvinist understanding of how a Christian church should be organized in freedom and order to the glory of God.

Our fathers confessed in 1788 that they were unanimously of the opinion that they considered

> . . . the rights of private judgment, in all matters that respect religion, as universal and unalienable . . . that, in perfect consistency with the above principle of common right, every Christian church, or union or association of particular churches, is entitled to determine the terms of admission into its communion, and the qualifications of its ministers and members, as well as the whole system of its internal government which Christ has appointed: that in the exercise of this right they may, notwithstanding, err, in making the terms of communion either too lax or too narrow; yet, even in this case, they do not infringe upon the liberty or the rights of others, but only make an improper use of their own . . . they are persuaded that there is an inseparable connection between faith and practice, truth and duty. Otherwise it would be of no consequence either to discover truth or to embrace it. . . . That while under the conviction of the above principle they think it necessary to make effectual provision that all who are admitted as teachers be sound in the faith, they also believe that there are truths and forms with respect to which men of good characters and principles may differ. And in all these they think it the duty both of private Christians and societies to exercise mutual forbearance towards each other. . . . That all church power . . . is only ministerial and declarative; that is to say, that the Holy Scriptures are the only rule of faith and manners; that no church judicatory ought to pretend to make laws to bind the conscience in virtue of their own authority; and that all their decisions should be founded upon the revealed will of God. Now though it will easily be admitted that all synods and councils may err, through the frailty inseparable from humanity, yet there is much greater danger from the usurped claim of making laws than from the right of judging upon laws already made, and common to all who profess the Gospel, although this right, as necessity requires in the present state, be lodged with fallible men. . . . That, if the preceding Scriptural and rational principles be steadfastly adhered to, the vigor and strictness of its discipline will contribute to the glory and happiness of any church. Since ecclesiastical discipline must be purely moral or spiritual in its object, and not attended with any civil effects, it can derive no force whatever but from its own justice, the approbation

of an impartial public, and the countenance and blessing of the great Head of the Church universal.

It is in the spirit of this great declaration that I have accepted this office. I stand before you as one who believes in a high doctrine of the Church. Christian faith and life is never a purely individual matter. Karl Barth recently, in an address to a conference on humanism, put the importance of fellowship and community on an even more universal basis when he eloquently said:

> Humanity is the fellowship of men. Where there is no fellowship there is inhumanity. We are human only in being together in a fellowship, seeing each other as men, hearing each other as men, talking with each other as men, helping each other as men, and doing all this with freedom because we like to do it.

A church (as a state, in the last analysis) is a voluntary fellowship of men who must decide in some way the rules by which they remain a fellowship. I therefore speak against that rampant individualism of either conservative or radical which lightly breaks the corporate fellowship of Church or State by words or acts however sincerely held to be the will of God. Tonight I would pledge to you, and through you to the whole body of our Church, to serve you all in accordance with the spirit and the law of the form of government of our inheritance. I do this because I delight to do so. Long ago I chose to serve my Lord within the Church and not independent of it. And despite all discouragements and frustrations no experience within our Church has led me to believe that there is any better way.

All this is based at last upon a faith, a bold faith that must always await God's consummations for its proof. It is the faith that the Spirit of God delights to guide the affairs of men, not only through the mystic inspiration of lonely prophets, but also and even more often through groups of men, who, with a common faith in Him, in the spirit of prayer and commitment to His will, in discussion and mutual forbearance, in the light of His word in the Scriptures, in listening to others and speaking out individual convictions, come at last to their decision which is more than their own decision and more likely to be the will of God than the individual insight of any single man. Yes, I boldly speak our faith: The Holy Spirit speaks through the actions and decisions of a presbytery.

I want to take a moment to return to the wider context of my subject and the beginning of this chapter. We Presbyterians believe that it was this bold faith that created and made workable the constitutional governments in Europe and the Western world that have had success in organizing freedom into the common life of men. James Hastings Nichols in his recent book *Democracy and the Churches* has pointed out what seems to me to be an important historical fact. It is in only those parts of the Western world where this faith was taken seriously (that God would find a better answer for a group of men in serious consultation than the individual genius or aristocrat or dictator could arrive at by himself) that representative government has worked at all. Unless there is this faith and this commitment, legislatures break into factions and committees do no more than pool their ignorances, and soon men give up their right to rule themselves for more efficiency. We live in a moment of history when the pressures of political and social problems are so critical that unless we really believe in representative democracy and make it work, our world will become once more totalitarian. The hope of a free Western world to bind men into a new unity of culture, faith, and all of life depends more than I like to think on the kind of faith in God and upon the kind of organization of government which we have inherited in our particular tradition. For the only freedom that can last is freedom under God, a disciplined freedom of men who voluntarily submit to their brethren because, as men, they delight so to do.

Chapter 2

THE VERTICAL DIMENSION
OF HISTORY*

DESPITE all of the anxieties and concerns which are shared by thoughtful Christians all over the world, the word of Jesus Christ to His Church and to His followers is "Be of good cheer, I have overcome the world." But to tell any one to be of good cheer in a day like ours at least raises some questions. The years since World War II was victoriously concluded have been years of disappointment and disillusionment. Long before we had the opportunity to clear up the debris—physical, financial, and spiritual—of that tremendous effort, we began to face the possibility of another war just as great or greater and with much less hope of a happy outcome.

The spiritual and idealogical structure of Christendom has been so badly shaken by the wars of the twentieth century that the strain of a third World War promises total and permanent collapse. The militarizing, brutalizing, spiritually degrading effects of another war, not to mention the loss of life and wealth entailed in it, would likely be more than Western civilization could survive.

If we are completely immersed in the stream of human history, there is little for man to be cheerful about. Only if we include another dimension to life besides the horizontal flow of history can there be found a true basis for Christian hope. God gives each moment in the flow of history a new look. A new perspective is added. Some of the confusion and all of the hopelessness is removed, and interest in God and the vertical dimension of history which His inclusion adds must not be substituted for the active and vital concern of Christians for what goes on in the ordinary affairs of the world. Jesus did not say, "Be of good cheer, the world is unimportant." It is always wrong to replace the horizontal

* The following essay was written in 1948.

measurements of history with the vertical. This is an ever present danger of any religious understanding of life. Ever and again, especially when events promise disaster, religious people are tempted to flee the world.

Jesus did not say, "Be of good cheer, things are not as bad as they look." A second and perennial danger of religion is to sentimentalize. It will do us no good to suppose that the historical issues we face are any less desperate than they appear.

Jesus said, "Be of good cheer, I have overcome the world." He had overcome the world because, although fully immersed in the stream of history, He had and offers a vital relationship to the eternal God, who is both the Lord of history and yet is also before and after, above and beyond all history. Our essential trouble is that we do not really believe in God. We talk about Him, we think we have adopted Him as our theory, but we are apt either to put Him off into the past or to hope for Him in some far-off future. But too often God seems to be nothing to us now. It was because of the realized presence of God that Jesus was able to say to his Disciples, "Be of good cheer, I have overcome the world."

Chapter 3

SKELETON IN THE CHURCH—
THE NEED FOR ORGANIZATION*

IT is often said that Christ, or anyone else, would have been somehow a better Christian if He had had no loyalties to any particular
company of the faithful and no convictions of any specific sort
about the truths of faith—all of which is of course nonsense. While
we may, as I do, deplore the divisions of the Church of Christ,
let us not make the egregious mistake of supposing that secondary
loyalty after our basic Christian loyalty is either unnecessary or
shameful. *Life* magazine put the matter much more wisely when
it concluded: "Happy is he who can find his religion within the
ancient wisdom of a Church; happy the nation."

Of course it is true that the organization of religion is not the
same thing as faith itself or worship. Of course it is true that the
depths of Christian experience are plumbed and the heights of
Christian experience are attained, not by majority votes or by
church executives in official edicts, but by individual "God-intoxicated" men and women.

But some would have us believe that it would be better if there
were no Church organizations at all; that to organize religion
destroys it; that though God is great and Christ is good, the
Christian Church, like all organized religion, is evil. It is in
direct opposition to this too-prevalent mood, even among professing Christians, that I speak to you on the "Skeleton in the Church,"
suggesting that without organization Christianity would be as
formless and futile as a body without its bones, as a man without
his spine and its attached and necessary appendages. I am speaking
against jellyfish religion in favor of a faith and Church which is

* The following sermon was given in 1949, while Dr. Blake was pastor of
a Pasadena church, and has as its text: "And in those days when the
number of the disciples was multiplied, there arose a murmuring. . . ."
(Acts 6:1–8).

15

unashamedly vertebrate. And to support my position I ask you to look with me at the incident in the very early history of the Christian movement.

Christianity had just begun that miraculous growth from a small company of discouraged Disciples into a vital movement that in a generation captured the attention of the whole Mediterranean world, in a few centuries became the dominant and official religion of the empire that had tried to destroy it, and in a thousand years survived the last vestiges of the empire itself and became the chief channel to our day of the cultural treasures of the ancient world, both secular and religious.

But look at the very beginning of that exciting story of the expansion of Christianity. The first Easter is just past. The discouraged eleven have been transformed into apostles, witnessing to the miracle of the Living Christ and winning men to His Lordship who had never known Him before his death. Beginning at Pentecost the success of Peter and James and John and the rest in winning converts to the way of the crucified and risen Jesus was no less than miraculous. These first Christians were "God-intoxicated men" all right. Accused of actual drunkenness on Pentecost, Peter proved that he had what a tired and thirsty world desired. Converts came and flocked to their company by the scores and hundreds. And thus far there was no church organization—just eleven leaders and increasing numbers of people. "Those of the Way" they were called. The leaders spoke when moved by the spirit of God and the people gathered to hear and pray.

Why didn't the Church stay that way, just informal gatherings under informal leadership of God-directed men and women? The answer is clear. There were responsibilities to each other that they all felt. Some were very poor, others at least relatively well off. So because of the spirit of Christ, they were impelled to share food with one another. At first it was easy. The apostles received and distributed it—they were a large but intimate and happy family. But notice the first verse of the sixth chapter of Acts: "And in those days when the number of the disciples was multiplied, there arose a murmuring. . . ."

I have cut off the verse arbitrarily at this point since the specific reason for the murmuring is comparatively unimportant. The sacred writer made clear his conviction that the cause of the murmuring was basically that the number of Christians had grown beyond what the organizationless Church could handle in the old informal way. Something had to be done about it, and the apostles met together to consider the problem. The cause of the murmurings was that some of the Christians, particularly those of gentile background, felt that in the daily food-sharing they were being overlooked in favor of the majority of Jewish background. This was serious even though the charge itself was likely groundless. But groundless or not, the apostles could not afford to have the brotherhood and unity of their company divided. Although there is no account of their discussion of the problem, we do have stated for us their decision. They must have agreed that there were now too many Christians for them to handle properly, especially in this daily giving out of food. They could not afford to give their whole time, as they said, to "serving tables," so neglecting their primary responsibility of spiritual leadership. " 'It is not reason that we should leave the word of God and serve tables.' "

There was only one thing they could do. I challenge anyone to suggest another. They had to begin the organization of the Church. Thus they said to the congregation that had been murmuring: " 'Look ye out among you seven men of honest report, full of the Holy Spirit and wisdom, whom we may appoint over this business.' " If organization in the Church is basically wrong, if organized religion is worse than, and essentially different from, pure religion, we will have to go way back there to the first few months of life of Christianity and find the source of the wrong in that decision of the apostles to extend the organization of the Church. For once begun, due to the increase of numbers in the first instance, organization must continue to grow as the numbers of Christians grow. That was why a little later, when the congregations got too big to handle, they were divided and soon such separate congregations needed supervision—hence presbyters and bishops. Some kind of organization was inevitable and necessary if the Church was to continue to grow and to come even close to retaining the spirit of its founder, Jesus Christ.

As the years and centuries passed there grew into the organization of the church evils, understandably human evils, but still evils, those of autocracy and totalitarianism, of irresponsibility and materialism, of selfish interests and unchristian competition for place and power. Some of the worst of these evils were attacked and in large part corrected in the Reformation. Others are with us yet in all branches of the Church, Catholic and Protestant. If the Church is to be Christian, there must be continual effort upon the part of every one of us to correct under God the evils and weaknesses that we now have and to watch closely to avoid any and all that may in the future threaten.

But the point that we must be perfectly clear about is whether the organization of the Church is right or wrong, whether it is worth struggling with or not, whether we would be better Christians if we sought God as individuals and separately tried to do his bidding in the spirit of Christ.

The answer of the Catholic part of the Church is abundantly clear on this. Salvation is in the Church alone. By the sacraments properly administered, by the historic Church through its appointed ministers alone does God give salvation to men. Their answer then to the question of organization is clear and unanswerable. There must be such organization to administer the sacraments.

But we Protestants do not believe that God is so limited in His power and sovereignty that He cannot save except through an official priest. "The spirit of God works when and where and how he pleases." Then why the organization of the Church? Because essentially you cannot be a Christian alone. It is where two or three at least are gathered in the name of Christ that He promises to be present in their midst. As Dr. Ganse Little has said: "Herein lies the only saving power the church possesses— the saving power of Christian fellowship"—not by magic sacraments, not by legalistic moralities, not by intellectual creedal isms, but by the fellowship of a dedicated and worshiping community.

If it is true that we need each other, in communities, intimate and loyal, to teach and to learn of God, to work at the tasks of the Kingdom, to share one another's burdens and joys, to reach out into the community and the world for Christ, then we must have organization to do it. If the Church is an amorphous mass, with no long arms to reach out and embrace the lonely and the lost, if it has no legs and feet to march forward, to capture new areas of life and territory for Christ, if it has no vertebrate structure to resist evil (organized well, it is), then today, as in the first century, we may be sure that the cause of Christ will stumble, fall, and die.

The trouble with our Presbyterian Church is not then that it is organized—no, not that. The trouble is that you and I have fatuously supposed for too long that it was not important whether it was organized or not. We have let the framework inherited from our fathers, wiser than we in this, creak and groan and become inadequate to its responsibilities in this world of today.

Two truths I would leave with you:

1. The organization of the church is important. "Good organization is necessary to keep out bad organization."

2. The church is an instrument and not an end—the instrument of God's glory.

Chapter 4

MILITANT FAITH—A WORD
TO CONSERVATIVES*

WHEN I was a small boy growing up in St. Louis in one of the
Presbyterian Sunday Schools, we used with great gusto to sing:
"Onward Christian soldiers, marching as to war, with the cross of
Jesus going on before." For a good many years now "Onward
Christian Soldiers" has not been a fashionable hymn to sing in
many church circles. The reason for this is the bad conscience
of many Christians as to their churches' failures in wartime to
make sufficient distinction between the nation's war effort and
the battle in which the churches themselves should be directly
engaged. Actually, there is nothing wrong and a good deal right
with the sentiment expressed in "Onward Christian Soldiers," if
you think about what the words really say. Note that the war
supported in the opening verse is the battle of the Church—
Christian soldiers are marching *"as to war"*—moreover there is
the "Cross of Jesus going on before," which symbolizes both the
purpose of this Christian war and even hints at its unique method
of victory—not by the infliction of suffering on an enemy, but
rather by the voluntary acceptance of suffering by the *Christian*
soldiers.

In this vein I have chosen the subject "Militant Faith—A Word
to Conservatives." I use this military metaphor, not in any connection whatever with the nation's present military effort in Vietnam, but to set the tone of what I want to say about the present
state of the Christian Church in our nation and in the world as
it is engaged in its battles both to survive and to be relevant to the
life of men and women everywhere.

"The Church Militant" is a traditional way to describe the
Christian Church theologically in "salvation history," between the

* This address was delivered in 1966.

coming of Christ almost two thousand years ago and His Parousia, or second coming in power to establish His Kingdom on earth. I do not want to discuss the theology of dispensationalism but to remind you that to think of Christians and the Church as an army of soldiers is on the whole right and useful.

The military metaphor reminds one of a number of spiritual truths that are always in danger of being forgotten. For example, there is a leader and commander, even Jesus Christ. Again there are powerful enemies who will be defeated only if, in addition to loyalty, there is strategy in our Christian efforts. Furthermore we need to remember that the Church is not essentially an institution but a movement. It has a mission in the military sense of that word, that is to say, an objective to be achieved, and there are adversaries who stand in the way of our reaching it. One can go on and be reminded of the discipline and organization required as much in an effective church as in an effective army. Further there is variety and diversity in any army. Some fight on the front lines, and others are engaged in bringing up supplies and support from the rear. There are skirmishers, cavalry, artillery, and even spies, as well as quartermasters, foot soldiers, cooks, physicians, and generals. One could go on in this way and remember too that unity is as important to the Church as it is to an army. Variety and diversity are as important, but no more so than coordination, discipline, and unified command.

I do not know how many of you may be chess players. In this age of television, it is my guess that few of us play chess very often. And let me make it clear at the outset that I do not speak about chess as an expert, but as a rank amateur. This much I have learned about this military game: after the formal opening, one soon finds himself both under attack and attacking. The king, and the other pieces too, must be constantly defended; but no victory can be won in chess unless you attack as well. The fun of the game is in the combination of the two purposes. Nothing is quite so pleasant as to find a defensive move, forced upon you by your opponent, which is at the same time offensive; that is, you put pressure upon a piece of your opponent's in the process of defending your own.

Or perhaps some of you are more familiar with football. A successful football team must be able to score itself and to keep down the score of the other team. One of the best ways to defend is what coaches call "ball control"—to keep on the attack for as many minutes of each quarter as possible. The best defense is often a good offense.

So much for illustrations. I want to discuss what the Church must defend and also what it must attack.

To do this, I must remind you first of the obvious fact that our world is a changing world. This has been said so often and in so many ways that it is hard to talk about it without boring you by repeating what you have heard too often already. So I shall merely use the common words to remind you of the extent and depth of the changes we face in our world. For it is, I believe, the number of changes that we face, plus their interplay on each other, that cause a great deal of the fear and frustration that characterize our times.

Population explosion—all over the world. What do we do to feed, house, and organize the life of men whose numbers are growing by geometric progression?

Urbanization. How do we keep human life human and humane, when men are more and more packed into high-rise apartments in bigger and bigger cities?

Technological unemployment. How do we find jobs for everybody when programmed machines do so many things better? And how do we use the leisure that machines make possible?

Depersonalization. How do we avoid becoming merely numbers in a machine?

Cybernetics. Who is to program the machines and with what values?

Nuclear war. How do we prevent it and how can we find ways to promote peaceful change?

The shrinking world. What does it mean that on radio we can hear and on television we can see immediately anything of importance wherever it happens?

Interdependence. What does it mean to be dependent for life itself on electricity or rapid transit or good labor relations?

Pluralism. How can you reconcile necessary tolerance with vital convictions?

I have said enough, I hope, to make it clear to all of us that our world is rapidly becoming a very different place from that into which most of us were born. Change is rapid and even revolutionary. And most of us don't like it. Our securities are threatened. We fear the future. We want to withdraw but find ourselves increasingly involved. What do Christians do in such a changing world? Is our faith relevant to any of this? My topic suggests that militant faith is relevant, that a battle is going on in this world of change and that the Church and its lay movements must join in the battle. And this battle is both defensive and offensive, as is every battle. I ask you now to consider with me two questions: What must we defend? And what do we attack?

What does militant Christian faith defend?

First of all we defend the faith itself. One of the reasons that conservative-minded Christians are so much upset with the world and with their own churches today is that they fear that the churches are listening so much to the secular world that they are giving up the essential reason for their existence, namely, God and the gospel—the good news of Jesus Christ. And this fear has some grounds. In every age there is the possibility that the essential values and goods of the past will be lost, or partly lost, in trying to adjust to the present and the future.

What are conservatives among us properly worried about? They are afraid that their ministers and leaders don't believe in God anymore. They are afraid that they don't believe in morality —in right and wrong. They are afraid that we don't believe the Bible, that there is no longer any authority. They are afraid that denominational leaders don't believe in their denominations, that they have given up on their congregations, and that the lay people are not heeded in their concerns.

Remember my point here is that militant faith will defend the truth and the values of the past. And my sincere answer to the conservatives of the Church is that it is important that we lose none of these things. It is, however, interesting to me that all of these fears, which I have already said are legitimate, had more ground when I was a boy in St. Louis fifty years ago than in my judgment they have today. Fifty years ago the Christian understanding of God as revealed in Jesus Christ in the Bible was more under attack than it is today, either in the world or in the Church itself. Darwin and evolution, technology (primitive though it was by our standards) and materialism, historical criticism of the Bible, and the whole idea of revelation were shaking the very foundations of the Christian faith in 1916 (when I moved away from St. Louis) in a way that none of these "new ideas," or their successors are doing today. The climax of that battle of defense came about 1926, forty years ago, and ever since, the Church has been stronger in a defensible faith than it had been since Darwin and the Industrial Revolution.

In another connection I have recently outlined what appears to me to be ecumenical consensus theology that has made the Church stronger in the past thirty years than it had been before. I repeat the four points here. The theology that now undergirds the churches, Protestant, Orthodox, and Roman Catholic, may be summed up in these four major convictions:

1. There is a transcendent God, who has revealed Himself in Jesus Christ.

2. Knowledge of this God is found in reading the Bible and understanding what it says in historical context.

3. The heart of Christian faith remains what it always has been. God, who created the universe, is Redeemer through Jesus Christ and He is fulfilling His purpose in history.

4. "Time makes ancient good uncouth," which fact requires us radically to revise our understanding of what should be expected of followers of Jesus Christ today as contrasted to what was required fifty years ago.

This is not an easy faith or a minimum faith. This is the traditional faith restated for our times. It is under attack from many quarters. It needs to be defended, not merely as a theoretical theology, but as the conviction by which Christians must live in order to be Christian soldiers. I would, therefore, remind those conservatives in the Church who are fearful that the faith is being betrayed by the Church itself that they often are attacking the wrong enemy when they are fundamentally critical of the ecumenical consensus that is guiding most of the churches in America today. As in a confused battle in a fog, it is not always easy to determine which is friend and which is foe, so today many fearful conservatives do not realize that the restatement of the ancient biblical faith and its defense is in fact the number one duty of the Church in our time.

In the second place, militant Christian faith in our times is called upon to defend the best of the heritage of our nation. I will mention just four aspects of our American heritage that I believe all Christians ought to join in defending:

1. *Equality*, especially equality of opportunity. The Declaration of Independence and the Constitution of the United States were written with the conviction that all men by their creation had rights. "Life, liberty, and the pursuit of happiness" is the classic formula. Totalitarian governments of both the left and right ignore and trample these basic rights of men. It is true that we have not as a nation always lived up to this initial faith and conviction. It took almost one hundred years for the nation to understand that the slavery of Africans was a contradiction to our basic national position. As we approach the end of the second hundred years, we confess these rights are still unsecured for all our people. We must as Christians defend the basic equality of all men as the pledge of allegiance expresses it, "with liberty and justice for all."

2. We must defend "responsible individual freedom." I have traveled a good deal in the past ten years in communist countries. The one thing we have that these totalitarian states do not have is individual freedom. If and when the power of any state is used to coerce men to think alike or to regiment their acts, the freedom which we as Christians must defend is lost. But our nation is lost if, generally speaking, this freedom is irresponsibly used. We must as Christians uphold responsible freedom.

3. We must defend individual enterprise. The strength of our nation is still in its voluntarism in business, in social concern, and in government. This is the importance of the YWCA, the Church, the trade union movement, the Chamber of Commerce, the women's clubs, and the whole galaxy of enterprise of our nation. The encouragement of free enterprise in this sense is one part of our heritage we must be in the business of defending.

4. Finally, as Christians, we must defend government of, by, and for the people. We are proud people and all pride is not evil. We should be proud of our great experiment of government, of its stability, its resiliency, and its justice. By no means have we been perfect. During most of our history, municipal government has been excessively corrupt. But we have institutions of freedom which we must defend. If we successfully defend our faith and our heritage in the terms in which I have stated them, we will have made the relevant contribution of faith to life that our times demand of us. I am pleading with you to be conservatives in this sense.

But to conserve the good of the past and to defend it requires us equally to attack—to lead in the offensive that militant Christian faith requires of us.

What then must we attack? I mention three enemies that we must defeat:

1. The too-prevalent conservative attitude that innovation is wrong per se. You will remember that I listed the new facts that we face in a changing and revolutionary world. To try to be conservative by ignoring the new conditions in which all men find themselves today and to resist for this reason the efforts to change anything is the new way to lose the battle. It is because we are conservative in the right sense that there must be innovations and risks undertaken.

The most exciting and rewarding things that have been happening in the life of the Church are precisely the new stances and activities that have been so controversial—nuns demonstrating in the streets for civil rights; ministers of comfortable churches with their young people actually risking their lives out of militant faith; ecclesiastical officials willing to risk the institution's unity and strength for the purpose of saving its soul.

These are the reasons it is good to be alive in the Christian movement today and I feel sorry for all those who, through fear or misunderstanding, have not become a part of it. It is new patterns of life conserving the values of the past that are the hope of the future.

2. Again we must attack hypocrisy, which is today, as it was two thousand years ago, the chief sin of religious people. I do not believe we ought to be easily charging all who disagree with us with hypocrisy. But I do suggest that we must attack root and branch those who profess Americanism and Christianity to cover up their major concern of holding on to special privilege. We will never successfully resist atheistic communism unless we stop using God to defend pocketbooks and privilege.

The Marxist charge is that all our institutions, including the Church, are but thinly disguised attempts to keep the masses of the people down in order that the privileged people may stay in control and protect their privileges. They charge that our laws do not aim at justice but rather at control. They say that our whole way of life is a gigantic hoax on the common people in the name of God.

I shall not take time to demolish this argument of the Marxist. It can be demolished. But it cannot ever be countered successfully in the world of today unless we who believe in freedom repent of our greed and turn from our personal fears and give up our hypocrisies.

In these past few years I have been giving a great deal of my time in the concerns of race and of poverty. I mention these two areas of present concern, because they are the best illustrations of the hypocrisy of the Church and nation which must be attacked in order to save the Church and nation.

Despite the clear teachings of the Christian gospel and the basic framework of the Constitution of the United States that racial prejudice and racial discrimination are utterly wrong, there are millions of Christian Americans who have not yet been brave enough to take their stand unequivocally for racial and economic justice. I do not charge any individual with conscious hypocrisy. That is not the issue. I do charge the groups of Americans who have not yet joined in the critical battle to establish equal justice, freedom, and opportunity for all in our land and in the world with the ultimate betrayal of the Church and nation in favor of fear and selfishness.

The slum housing in New York, Chicago, Los Angeles, Philadelphia, Detroit, Cleveland, Boston, Baltimore, and St. Louis is a disgrace to the nation and will be the cause of its collapse unless we tear the tenements down and build decent housing for the poor. The educational system, which gives poor education to the poor, must be supported by more dollars than any legislation has yet dreamed of so that we can safely retain government of and by the people. The health of the poor in this rich land is a disgrace to any people. The racial discrimination in jobs, the level of wages in the worst jobs (I refer to migrants, tenant farmers, service employees, domestics, etc.) give grounds for the Marxist charges against our whole way of life.

You will note that I have not used the words capitalism or socialism. I suggest that they are used mostly to confuse the social and economic issues that the nation and the world are facing and to prevent answers being found. What I am saying, and

I hope very clearly indeed, is that we must attack hypocrisy which uses any kinds of words to cover up hate and fear and greed.

3. Finally, I suggest that we must attack that blighting cynicism which takes the heart out of the troops. This is where the Church has a very specific contribution to make in the course of this battle. To believe in God is to have courage in the face of defeat. To follow Jesus Christ is not to be a romantic idealist but to believe despite the sin of man, realistically observed, that men may be converted by the power of God. To be a Christian is to believe that with God the battle may be won in this world now and in eternity.

The blight of cynicism, which leads to distrust of one another and saps the courage of us all, is an enemy that must be defeated.

So I have tried to encourage the Church to militant faith to defend and cherish what is good, to attack and destroy what is evil. Such faith gives meaning to human life and hope to a revolutionary and changing world. God grant us all this kind of faith.

Contemporary
Pressures

Chapter 5

POVERTY IS EMBARRASSING*

IF American Christians don't come to grips with the gospel soon, increasingly men of good will not only will reject the Church, but much more important they will reject Jesus Christ and Him whom He came to earth to reveal.

The problem is that many Americans most sincerely believe in God, Jesus Christ, and the Bible, while at the very same time they live and act as if God had not made them, as if Jesus Christ had never come to earth, and as if they had never read the Bible at all.

At a small seminar which I attended last month, one careful observer of twentieth-century American life commented that our problem is that modern Americans have taken the list of the seven deadly sins of the Middle Ages and accepted them as outlining a realistic reading of human nature. If our Madison Avenue advertisers do in fact know what will appeal to the American people and what will motivate us to buy their products, their advertisements indicate that this observer was right.

How many Buicks have been sold this year on snob appeal? (Envy) How many cake mixes have been sold by pictures of cakes covered with globs of drooly icing? (Gluttony) Why do partly clad women appear in ads selling everything from pencils to mink? (Lust) Why is insurance sold so often on the basis of a young man's status? (Pride) Have you ever read the copy designed to lure you into a fling at the stock market? (Avarice) What is the pitch basic to the campaigns of many household labor-saving devices? (Sloth) How do we stir up the American people's patriotism but by hatred of other peoples? (Anger)

I am not pointing the finger at any of you more than at myself.

* This sermon was delivered in 1964 and has as its text: " 'Blessed are you poor, for yours is the Kingdom of God' " (Luke 6:20).

The fact is we are all in trouble as severe as that of St. Paul when he wrote, "Wretched man that I am, who will deliver me from the body of this death? . . . I do not do the good I want, but the evil I do not want is what I do."

But we are really in a worse case. Paul was clear as to what was evil and what was good. Our twentieth-century Christianity is infected by the disease of an almost complete reversal of standards as to what is really good.

All this I set forth as introductory to a consideration of one of the New Testament's texts most embarrassing to American Christians today. These words of Jesus as found in Luke 6:20: " 'Blessed are you poor, for yours is the Kingdom of God.' " Who of us is not embarrassed by these almost incomprehensible words of our Lord? Jesus says flatly to poor people: "You are the happy ones, God and heaven are yours." The communist says to us all: "Yah, that *is* Christianity—sell pie in the sky to the also-rans in society so they won't revolt." That's embarrassing to us all, isn't it? The so-called evangelical says to the advocate of the "social gospel": "It is clear your programs of social welfare are precisely the opposite of true Christian spirituality. Besides, Jesus said that we will always have the poor with us." To which the so-called liberal Christian replies: "You fundamentalists who insist on taking the whole Bible literally and of equal inspiration, how do you justify the middle-class virtues you extol in the face of 'Blessed are you poor, for yours is the Kingdom of God' "?

Even the poor man himself is embarrassed. "Maybe my poverty is a gate to spiritual blessing, but, in the words of that popular and profound 1964 song lyric, I must say, 'Having seen which is which, I'd rather be rich.' " And how embarrassing is my text to Sargent Shriver, the head of the federal government's "Anti-Poverty Program." If poverty is the basis of spiritual and eternal good, why should it be eliminated in a "Great Society"?

The only Christian who would not find this text embarrassing, I judge, would be a twentieth-century St. Francis of Assisi, who, you remember, turned away from the security and relative comfort of his home and family and actually embraced poverty voluntarily as his way of life. There have been a few of these from age to age in each generation and generally they are venerated as "saints" by the rest of us. I remember meeting Miss Muriel Lester thirty years ago. She was an English woman, heiress to a considerable fortune from her family, who refused flatly to accept her inheritance and directed it, with some legal difficulty, to the alleviation of poverty in the east end of London.

But most of us, while admiring such saints, do not emulate them in their radical and naive response to Jesus' words.

Since, then, Jesus' words are, it appears, embarrassing to us all, will you not examine with me as objectively as we can what ought to be the attitude of American Christians toward poverty, both as it exists in our affluent nation and throughout the world at the end of this year of our Lord 1964?

The most Christian of all the Christmas greetings which I have seen this year was the editorial in the Christmas issue of the Jesuit magazine *America*. It read in part:

> The man who has everything doesn't much need our greeting. Millions of others do.
>
> If, in a unique way, Christmas is for children, it is also for the poor and suffering. . . . So, ahead of all others we greet the poor—the down-and-out, the anguished poor: those who won't get a single Christmas card or be able to afford a Christmas dinner, those whose relief checks were used up before Christmas Eve, those who owe big bills to doctors and spend Christmas wondering how to pay them, or who sit cheerless and alone on Christmas in chilly rented rooms, thinking of better times and remembering the faces of those who are dead. Then, too, we greet all who are down on their luck and on their nerve, who have lost faith and hope, who drift through the streets at Christmas, panhandling for a few drinks, who haven't any place to go and wouldn't be let in if they had. And, a special greeting goes to those who spend the Day when He was born cursing the day when they were born. Christ be with them.
>
> . . . So, greetings and love to the poor of Africa, India, Latin America, the Soviet Union, China, Europe, the whole globe. To the poor in Harlem, the southside of Chicago, the slums of a hundred big cities here and abroad—Christ be with you on Christmas day. The sick, hungry, lonesome, disturbed, embittered and abandoned—all those with big holes in their soles, and bigger holes in their hearts: we send you, not just these clichés of verbal blessing, but the love of Christ.

And the greeting concludes: "Compelled by that love, what are we doing to prove we are really your brothers in Christ? What are we going to do to prove it, all through 1965?"

Here then are the questions of this sermon, my affluent Christian friends: Compelled by the love of Christ, what are we doing to prove we are really the brothers in Christ of the poor? What are we going to do to prove it, all through 1965?

The traditional response of individual Christians and of the Christian Church to poverty has been caught up in that basically beautiful but now debased word "charity."

However inadequate to human need may be the individual outgoing response of the Christian to the poor persons whom he sees or knows, however pitiful and futile appear the sum total of all the good all Christians and all humanitarians together accomplish through their charitable organizations compared to the increasing hunger and poverty throughout the world, nevertheless, the first word of obedience to the gospel to us all in our comfort and relative affluence remains: to respond generously in love to human need of whatever kind and however caused.

This response of charity in the true sense is a mark of the presence of God in the world. When John the Baptist sent some of his followers to ask Jesus whether He was indeed God's anointed one to come, Jesus' reply, you remember: "Go and tell John what you hear and see, the blind receive their sight and the lame walk, lepers are cleansed and the deaf hear, and the dead are raised up, and the poor have good news preached to them." From the order of climax of Jesus' reply, it appears that he thought that preaching truly good news to the poor required a greater miracle than to raise the dead. And so it sometimes seems.

But let us not belittle the importance of Christians generously supporting the various programs and institutions of the Church and of others which have been set up to serve men in need. I visited last summer, under Christian Church sponsorship, two homes in Hungary; one where the old live out their years in peace and dignity, and the other where men and women give themselves each day to take care of mentally retarded children who will never be able to care for themselves. These homes were established by Christians in the name of Christ and continue because you and others give in charity to the Division of Interchurch Aid, Refugee and World Service of the World Council of Churches.

I have visited a hospital in Pakistan where the blind literally receive their sight by the power of Jesus Christ and the skill of devoted doctors and nurses. I have seen people in North Africa and Latin America who would have starved by now but for the surplus food American Christians have made available through Church World Service. I have visited a leper hospital in Nigeria where people who were without hope literally are given new life in the name of Christ. 1369049

I must not use up my time in describing this work further, for this is not a promotional sermon. But I remind you of Jesus' solemn parable of the rich man and the beggar at his gate. Both men died. The beggar was comforted in Abraham's bosom, and the rich man suffered the torments of hell. Why? Not because he was rich, but because his heart was cold and callous. He passed by the beggar at his gate—he didn't respond, he didn't even see him as the dogs licked his sores. Let nothing I say then give aid or comfort to any professing Christian or any Christian church which, in affluence, absolute or relative, cuts back the response of heart and hand in charity to simple human need. Humanitarianism is not a bad word in the Christian vocabulary. Our response to Christ in this respect is of ultimate significance. Remember the cup of cold water at the Judgment Day and the story of the rich man and Lazarus. Forget not charity.

But it is perfectly clear that charity in its traditional forms and expressions is not enough and can even be a salve to a conscience that ought to be stabbed awake.

We profess to be a Christian country. We are by all odds the wealthiest people that ever have lived. We have more things than men ever before have been able to accumulate to minister to comfort, amusement, and most outlandish desires. We gather in this most beautiful church, well dressed, well fed, and filled with euphoria. Yet less than a mile away, down from the heights, are rat-infested tenements, a ghetto of the poor, that would be a disgrace to a poor nation or a bankrupt people.

What can we do? Clearly the challenge is for the American people politically to change the economic rules of our society so that pockets of abject poverty are eliminated. I am weary of comfortable Americans using partisan political and economic arguments as excuses why nothing should be done. I am even wearier of Christians using spiritual excuses that life is more than food and clothes and shelter to justify themselves for voting selfishly and in fear of losing their own economic security or advantage.

The time has come, it is long overdue, for this people to

mobilize capital, private and public, to eliminate poverty. And if you say to me that no amount of capital can create the real answers to the problems of the poor, their hopelessness, their crime, their envy, and their anger, I will agree, but at the same moment remind myself and us all that to go on as we are with the economic rules unchanged, which permit me to make more money in a few months on the stock exchange with a bit of capital than poor families with both parents working hard all year can earn to feed their children, is neither Christian nor decent.

I confess that it is not easy to outline the programs of legislation that will meet these problems. Much less easy will it be to carry them out. But it seems to me abundantly clear that unless the American people begin to press business, trade union, university, and government leadership to treat our poverty as a moral issue, our culture and our nation ultimately will collapse in a swamp of greed and crime.

Envy, I admit, is as deadly a sin as avarice or sloth. But let no man rest complacent in America until as a people we have found the way to eliminate our poverty.

One other word must be said from the perspective of the Christian gospel. To achieve a better distribution of the necessities of life for all Americans of all races and colors is not enough.

The fact is that daily the wealthy nations as a group are growing wealthier and the poor nations as a group are growing poorer. Within five years, we are warned, basic famine will be permanently widespread in many parts of the world due to population growth and lagging agriculture that is the result of poverty. I am not impressed by those who keep counseling the American people that the only ground of foreign policy is self-interest, however enlightened. Unless we make a moral issue of our American poverty and go on to see the moral issue involved in the relations of our nation to the needy peoples of the whole world, let us not profess Christian faith, nor even humanitarian concern. Let us give up hypocrisy and admit we look out for ourselves alone. As Christian charity knows no limits, neither can Christians allow the artificial barriers of national boundaries to limit their moral concern for the worldwide problem of poverty.

Again, the solution of the problem is not a simple one. Again, I do not profess, nor should the church profess, to provide the necessary economic and political blueprint from a pulpit. But this we must proclaim. Jesus Christ died for the whole world and God's family includes all the peoples of this earth. We must remember these things when we write our congressmen and take our political positions.

Finally, I must remind you of the ultimate embarrassment of poverty. While we must strive to alleviate its effects and so far as possible to eliminate it, we who are affluent dare not forget other solemn words of Jesus. We dare not forget, we who are rich, that he said, "It is easier for a camel to pass through the eye of a needle, than for a rich man to enter into the Kingdom of God."

This is not a scolding of the rich. It is rather Jesus' clear-eyed warning to us. And the depth of the warning is brought home to us in an incident in the gospel which reads almost like a parable.

A young man of great possessions approached our Lord and we are told that Jesus looked on him and loved him. Jesus simply asked him to sell his possessions, to give the money to the poor, and to follow Him. How embarrassing it is for you and equally for me even to recall that incident. How can it be interpreted? Does it mean that Jesus says literally to each of us with possessions that this is what we should do?

I do not intend to weaken the force of this by interpreting it away. I do suggest that Jesus asked that particular young man to cut himself loose from his possessions, the things that threatened to enslave him, and to follow Him. I take the invitation to the young man most literally. He was invited to become one of the intimate followers of Jesus, perhaps one of the apostles, one of the twelve.

And he turned away, sorrowful, for he had great wealth. That is, Christian friends, precisely what threatens us all, individually and as a nation—that we will allow our possessions to stand in the way of truly abundant life.

For I return at the end of the sermon to those strangely disturbing and embarrassing words of Jesus which are my text: "Blessed [that is, happy] are you poor, for yours is the Kingdom of God." Can we believe Him? If we believe Him, will we follow Him into life truly abundant? Or will our great possessions make us at last and decisively turn away in sorrow?

Chapter 6

STRATEGY FOR A FREE WORLD*

MY subject today is suggested by the basic metaphor of war, which we use in the expression "*War* Against Poverty," and by that which we have also used to describe our own organization and activity: "Citizens' *Crusade* Against Poverty."

•   •   •

The enemy against which we wage our crusade is poverty. Let us be entirely clear that the enemy is not our political opponents, or economic rivals, or anyone who may be resisting the program or programs we support. Perhaps the greatest blind spot in the American people as they determine their government's policy, both domestic and foreign, is that they seem to see only one enemy, namely, communism and the men and governments which support it. As you shall see, I recognize this communism as the live alternative to the free world to which all of us here are committed, but the decades of American power will lead us and the world to great disaster unless more Americans quickly see that there are three polarizations dividing men in our world. It is no longer simply the problem of containing communism. The first polarization is still communist vs. the free world. But a second polarization everywhere equally important is racial: white vs. nonwhite. This is why the civil rights movement must not stop moving. And there is a third polarization equally divisive: rich vs. poor. In a meeting of the Central Committee of the World Council of Churches held in Switzerland in February, this new complexity became completely clear. One of the most articulate spokesmen from the Church in Eastern Europe, which is now well

---

* The following address was delivered April 13, 1966, in Washington, D.C., to the Citizens' Crusade Against Poverty, a coalition of nongovernmental organizations and citizens headed by Walter P. Reuther, president of the United Automobile Workers. Dr. Blake is one of six vice-chairmen.

represented in the World Council of Churches, in the debate on international relations said, "I was in the far East not long ago. I found that they no longer accept me as their spokesman." Turning to his fellow Europeans in the West, and to us Americans, he said, "These Asians said to me that I belonged with you and not with them. They said to me, 'You're rich. You're white. You belong with them.' " We are here because we recognize that besides communism and racial discrimination, poverty is an enemy that must be defeated if we are to have a free world.

The enemy in our crusade, however, is not personal. Poverty is a concept, but more than a concept, it is a human condition in which many men and women find themselves in our world of 1966. It is not adequately described as simple lack of goods or money, although such lack is indeed poverty's physical description. The poverty we fight is an involuntary, unwanted lack of the necessities for a good life, imposed upon some of our fellow human beings by the environment in which they find themselves. I take it no one here would want to eliminate that *voluntary* poverty freely accepted by some of the religious, and even by a few of the nonreligious, as part of their witness against the materialism of either Church or world.

No, the poverty we would eliminate is that imposed upon some persons and groups of persons in our society by its very pattern and rules. Furthermore, most have understood poverty as a spiritual condition, positively evil, which develops among those who have long been deprived of the necessary physical goods of life, or who receive a minimum of them in such ways as to be deprived also of their human dignity. It may very well be that the most difficult aspect of the war against poverty will turn out to be, not economic, but psychological—psychological, not only with respect to the ingrained attitudes of "the poor," but also with respect to the built-in psychological attitudes of those of us who by inheritance, or hard work, or good fortune (or a combination of these) are economically free in our politically free society. If it is true that some of the poor (e.g., some Negroes in the central cities and some whites in Appalachia) have developed an apathy or cynicism which makes them unable to struggle out of their poverty, whatever economic opportunities are opened to them, it is also true that most of the rest of us have developed a "syndrome of success," which separates us as much from sympathy with the poor, and understanding of their condition, as the "poverty syndrome" unfits the poor for successful competition in our kind of a free society.

My purpose is to help us all clarify our motives and means as we struggle for the elimination of poverty. And as I try to describe the strategy in this war for a free world, such strategy must be seen clearly in contrast to the communist strategy to the same end. Please note that I am taking seriously the worldwide communist effort to battle with the same enemy, namely, poverty. This is in contrast to all those in our country and in the free world who see communist ideology *only* as an enemy of freedom, and as the *only* enemy of freedom. As a churchman, I do not need to be reminded that when men of the Marxist faith come to power anywhere in the world the Church is attacked, its faith in God is ridiculed, and, although it survives, its life is severely curtailed. Equally you are involved in the trade union movement; some of you, having battled and suffered to keep your unions free from communist takeover, or domination, do not need to be reminded that Marxist ideology as it has worked out in the communist world is as inimical to the free trade union as it is to the Church. These things I say to make it evident that the managers and beneficiaries of capitalist enterprise are not the only ones in our society who have specific reason to resist communist ideology.

But, when communism is conceived as the *only* enemy of freedom, free men are betrayed—as we are in extreme danger of being beguiled—into defending any kind of effort, so long as it is successful, toward the defeat of the forces of communism. Because, however, many of our conservative Americans are so fearful of communism that they sincerely believe that all of us who are trying to influence our nation and government toward more equitable social and economic patterns of life are communists, communist sympathizers, or communist dupes, I shall take a moment to make it clear why I, at least, believe that the war against poverty, as we are engaged in it, is the only rival of communism that has any chance of success today. Let me then simply contrast the free world ideology, which I support, with the communist ideology, which is its active rival in the whole world today.

Communism is atheistic. The free world ideology is based upon faith in God as He has been known in the Judeo-Christian tradition. I mention this contrast first, not because I am a preacher, and could be expected to speak for God, but because I believe that faith in God is the only stable ground on which to build a just and free society. Men who reject a transcendent God usually come at last, or in the crisis, to worship themselves and so lose all drive for justice or freedom against their own self-interest.

The second contrast between communist ideology and that of the free world has to do with the understanding of man. Communism on the one hand idealizes man—if he is a worker—and on the other hand believes that no man, even a worker, has any right against the state. The free world, in contrast, informed by its religious tradition, recognizes each man realistically as selfish and sinful, but potentially as a child of God. Communism, therefore, believes it is right to liquidate all men who have property and disagree with its program, whereas the free world believes that men can be won to support, or accept, a more just society. Both, however, run the risk of romantic utopianism and both run the risk of cynical betrayal.

In the third place, communism puts all power and planning in a single place—the state. But the ideology of a free world depends upon there being multiple places of planning and decision—individual enterprise, the state, voluntary groups, trade unions, and business corporations, large and small.

And communism recognizes only material values, whereas we believe that the good life does not consist merely in the abundance of goods. "Bread *and* Roses" expressed it best on a striking picket's sign half a century ago in Pennsylvania.

Finally, communism believes in class warfare as the way to its utopia, whereas the free world holds that it is possible to build a community in which the enemy is not other men, but rather the pattern of evil itself which ought to be destroyed.

I make this summary, which I don't expect all of you to accept, as a ground for the program, in which we are all involved, as voluntary organizations in American life, to fight against poverty in this nation and in the world within the best tradition of a free society. And I call upon conservative Americans to support our effort on their own ground of freedom, lest all of us find ourselves in a world increasingly dominated by communism, tyranny, and materialism.

But is not this hope I express a romantic dream? Can we really believe that a free world strategy can succeed in competition with a ruthless communist conspiracy worldwide in scope? I have an advantage over some of you in this. I believe in God. But, aside from general theological grounds of hope, let us look for a moment at what is going for us even in this discouraging world of 1966. There are three grounds of hope which I shall mention.

1. We have the tradition and the fact of a representative government which is committed to equality and freedom and, further, to the welfare of the whole people. The stability of our free institution of government and its ability to respond to the changes in the technology and in the human expectations of our time is a tremendous force for orderly change. If I understand the basis of the coalition of voluntary groups that make up this Crusade Against Poverty, we support the efforts of federal, state, and local government, to establish laws and conditions which encourage the people to gain prosperity and security for themselves and also those which will serve the needs of all of our people who require community assistance in that struggle. Recognizing that there are and will be criminals and loafers in every society, nevertheless we support that kind of government that will by law and its execution curb the criminal, stimulate the lazy, and support the weak. Believing that private property is a protection of freedom, we support government which controls the use of that property to the needs of the whole society.

2. A second ground of hope is the competence of the American people in solving the problems of science and engineering, of government and education, of production and distribution, which are before us. Though there is much ignorance to be overcome and much waste of the talent that is available, nevertheless we are blessed by the technical competence at all levels of our society. We know how to do what must be done once we decide to do it.

3. The third ground of hope is perhaps best symbolized by your presence here in this crusade. Our American tradition has encouraged voluntary and private efforts of a sometimes bewildering variety to do things that need to be done, to support the weak, to educate the ignorant, to set ideal goals, and voluntarily to work for them. This is a moral force in our society that must not become discouraged. There is, I know very well, a great deal of cynicism abroad in the land. But let us not forget that your presence here is proof of an amazing amount of unselfish devotion to a better world and a better life for all sorts and conditions of men.

We need these grounds of hope in order to go forward with courage in our attempt to eliminate poverty from this nation and at the same time to assist all the nations to find a way to peace, based upon justice, freedom, and their increasing prosperity. Let me then emphasize what our crusade is designed to do concretely:

1. We are a free coalition of national organizations committed to supporting at every level of government those laws, programs, and their administration which will eliminate from our land bad housing, bad education, racial and other discrimination, under-employment, and the irresponsible use of wealth and property. This does not mean all the organizations here represented will agree about all legislation and will become a giant lobby for any specific program. But we do agree, I believe, that we will resist those efforts upon the part of selfish interests to prevent all social legislation and its necessary development. We are one in resisting those who suppose that communism can be defeated simply by the war effort in southeast Asia, and who would, therefore, devote all American resources to it and thereby neglect, or strangle, or starve the war against poverty.

The free processes that have been established by the crusade to give each organization represented here the facts about the legislative problems and an opportunity to come to the support of just and needed governmental programs are designed both to protect the integrity of each of us and at the same time be a source of mutual strength and assistance toward our common goals.

2. Even more concretely, I call to your attention the crusade's announced program to train one thousand community leaders of the poor over the next few years in order that good leadership may enable the poor themselves to fight against the poverty that holds them down. I believe the plan that has been developed will meet the greatest unmet need in the war against poverty. The federal legislation has wisely determined that antipoverty efforts to be successful require participation, up to maximum feasibility, of the poor themselves. But the natural leaders of the poor need to be helped to lead. Unless we succeed in this concrete effort to recruit and train such community leaders in considerable numbers, the vacuum will be filled by self-serving exploiters of the poor, by ineffective and frustrated men of good will, or worst of all, by communists who do not want a free society to succeed. Our program is well conceived to produce effective leaders of the poor

who will be committed to a free society and who will know when to resist and when to conciliate, when to protest and when to negotiate, to the end that the American people together may win this war against poverty and not lose their freedoms in the process. There can be no real consensus unless the poor have better and more articulate leadership. We can help recruit and train it.

3. Already the crusade has established an information service, informing grass roots groups of the poor throughout the nation about the programs and opportunities that will help them to become effective in this antipoverty war. The poor themselves very often are the last to know about their opportunities to get out of poverty. More than four thousand such grass roots groups have been identified already, with additions to the list coming in each day and week. Most of these groups are in addition to the local branches of the national organizations represented here in the Crusade. Accurate information to the poor is a crucial part of our present program.

4. This information service is the beginning of the establishment of a national network of the poor themselves, who must be helped to help themselves get out of poverty. So the crusade is committed in line with government policy to recruit and organize the poor to engage in the war which must be won if America is to be both a force and an example in a free and prosperous world.

If we lose this war, it is clear that communists will be the winners in the competition for the support of the "third world" in Asia, Latin America, and Africa. The strategy for a free world depends upon the American people daring to change their own society soon enough and deeply enough that the hopes of our own American Revolution of nearly two hundred years ago shall be realized for all men and for ourselves. And I remind you, as I conclude, that the enemy we fight is poverty itself. We seek in a free society to do what others would do by the methods of dictatorship and tyranny.

Let us be not only the voice to articulate our hope, but the leaders and the troops who alone can win this war.

Chapter 7

WHAT IS A COMMUNITY? *

I COME to you today with a plea to abolish the Interracial Commission in Pasadena . . . but not yet! I want to do away with it just as soon as we have made enough progress in including our racial minorities in our community so that the need for an Interracial Commission will no longer exist. But until that day comes, I suggest to you that the Interracial Commission, which is reporting informally to you through me today, is a most vital part of the social machinery of this council and of this community.

Many of you have received from time to time reports of what this commission had done or was doing. These accomplishments of the past five years have not been inconsiderable. Although much remains to be done in every area, there have been significant advances in each of the areas into which our work has fallen: 1. educational encouragement; 2. employment assistance in both public and private enterprise; 3. recreation development; 4. hospitalization and medical care; 5. and even finally, I venture to say in housing, although in this area much of our progress has been of that negative kind the only result of which is that we now know more things that cannot be done than we did before.

But it seemed more to the point to me today to omit consideration of our accomplishments or our failures. I have decided not to direct your attention to what we have done but rather to what we have been; not to what we ought to do but to what we ought to be. For it is common European criticism of much of American life and culture that we are entirely too much inclined to be

---

* The following address was delivered January 13, 1948, to the Council of Social Agencies of Pasadena, California. At that time Dr. Blake, then pastor of a Pasadena church, was chairman of the local Interracial Commission.

activists whether in religion or in other social matters. And while as Americans we may properly not accept this criticism of ourselves at its face value, we may well admit that it is a good discipline for us to stop being so much impressed by our own busyness and to take more time to examine our state of being.

Five years ago the Council of Social Agencies here in Pasadena established its Interracial Commission. Its official purpose is:

> To uphold and promote human fellowship and harmony through mutual consideration and recognition of, and through respect for, all groups in the community;
> To strive to discourage in our community all animosities arising from the differences among racial groups, and to unite them in the fair play of civilized life;
> To champion human dignity and betterment, and to advance them without distinction of race, color, or creed.

To succeed in this purpose it is clear that we must find a way to reduce and eliminate racial tension in our community. But racial tension is a complex phenomenon that arises in racially diverse communities from a wide variety of causes—economic, political, social, cultural, and religious. Because of this great variety of its causes, racial tension is a social condition hard to combat, requiring as it does for its reduction or elimination: economic reform, political adjustment, social change, education of thought patterns, and better religion.

But I am convinced that there is one basic underlying cause of racial tension from which all these others are derivative: Racial minorities usually are not and do not feel themselves to be fully a part of the community. This lack of belonging is a more basic reason for racial tensions than any particular negative condition that affects minority life. I mean this: in such a community as ours, all of us are from time to time minorities. That is to say, the Board of City Directors does things from time to time that you or you and I are against. The Board of Education inevitably takes some actions against minority protests. The Council of Social Agencies can never have 100 percent support of all its actions and policies. But at other times and much more often in Pasadena most of us find ourselves in accord with the actions and policies of these important civic groups, and from time to time we may have the thrill of helping influence decisions in the direction of our convictions. In a democracy the minority on any specific issue has the right of agitation for reversal, education for a later better day, and appeal to higher bodies and to the courts if the action is unjust.

But suppose you found yourself in what seemed to you to be a permanent minority position, where your voice and vote were seldom if ever effective, where the majority against you was large enough to ignore you, your opinions, your rights, and your protests.

Now, I am not suggesting that racial minorities in Pasadena have no votes, no powers, no influence. We have here an effective political democracy. We have courts whose aim and practice is to protect all citizens equally before the law. But I suggest to you that a vote and rough justice from police and courts are not enough to make anyone fully a part of a community.

Certainly I need not argue the point before this audience (a voluntary association of men and women interested in and responsible for the many social institutions that grow up in a free society) that a good community is dependent upon voluntary as well as governmental agencies, churches, chambers of commerce, social service, and youth agencies, schools, health departments, recreation bodies, etc. It is the development of a myriad variety of such groupings that gives flavor and tone to any community. Our sense of belonging comes at last from our active participation in these associated activities.

But the fact is that members of minority races do not fully "belong" in the community of Pasadena as now organized. Do we not of the majority, for example, usually put the question thus when we discuss minority races: "What ought we do *for* Negroes or Spanish-Americans, or Orientals?" In a true community really inclusive of all its people, the question would be: "What shall we do *with* these people?" and I use that preposition in its proper meaning of "together with." Or to avoid any possibility of misunderstanding, the question should be put: "How shall we as a community of different races solve our personal and social problems of human relationships?"

I said at the beginning of this address, "abolish the Interracial Commission . . . but not yet." When? Only when racial minorities are so much an accepted part of the whole community that there is no need for a commission devoted to the special interests and special problems of these fellow citizens.

Let me be very concrete. There are businessmen and real estate men of minority races in Pasadena—Negroes, Japanese, Chinese —but few if any of these belong to our mercantile or trade associations. Now I am not saying that racial minority interests ought to dictate the policies of these or any of our official or voluntary civic groupings. I am saying merely that until the minority races are an accepted part of all our community civic, social, business, and cultural enterprises, they will be a problem to themselves and to the community and will need the services of an Interracial Commission and many other special efforts as well.

At the time when members of minority races are in all our thinking (majority and minority) an accepted part of the general membership and of the policy-making boards of our many city-wide voluntary and semigovernmental organizations, then and only then will there be no need for special organizations designed to give them voice and influence in our community. Some progress toward this goal has been made. The Council of Social Agencies itself, the Council of Churches, the YWCA, and many others of our community groups have already taken this step. But it must be admitted that by and large what we do in Pasadena is still apt to be *for* rather than *with* the racial minorities among us.

I am, of course, merely arguing here for social democracy as the solution to the problems created by racial variety in this or any community. This is not an easy solution. It is slow, sometimes exasperatingly slow. It requires the development of democratically chosen and proved leadership whom the community will follow. It requires the give and take of legitimate compromise. It requires a clear vision of the goal we seek combined with persistent patience in moving toward it.

What are the alternatives? Some few would argue for a permanent segregated and secondary position for racial minorities in America. These would argue that the system in vogue in our Southern states is really better for the Negro in that there he knows his place (for he has a place) in the community and is therefore not subject to the kind of frustration he meets in the North or West where ideally he is a full participating citizen but where actually after graduating from the nondiscriminating public schools he finds himself in a society that really has no place for him. While we may admit some of the force of the Southern argument, it is unthinkable that America should reverse the direction she has chosen from her earliest history and revert to a system of master and slave, patron and client.

Some would argue that another alternative would be to go on about as we are, and their chief reason for opposing advance toward a fuller social democracy is that minority races do not and cannot produce capable leaders trusted by their constituencies. This charge must be answered. In the first place we should acknowledge that the producing of able leaders by the majority race in our democracy is, to say the least, not 100 percent satisfactory. Again we need to be reminded that there is no scientific basis whatever in anthropology which would support the idea that minority races are inherently incapable of producing leaders and following them. And finally it needs to be said that there is but one way to produce leaders and that is to give them responsibility to lead. I am reminded of what used to be said by men in justification of the British rule in India. It was often claimed that the Indian people were incapable of producing leaders and the example given was that there were not natives in the Indian army capable of being more than junior officers. The devastating reply to this argument was given by an Englishman, a student of history, who had lived long in India. He admitted that it might be true that at the moment in India there were no able Indian officers. But if true, he argued that this was the final proof of the degenerating influence of imperialism itself, for he reminded his fellow British that when they were conquering India the Indians had then some very able generals indeed. In fact, Rangit Singh, the Lion of Lahore, had about succeeded in defeating entirely the British armies trying to "pacify" the Punjab.

There is only one way to produce leaders and that is by providing opportunity for them to lead. And although we have no right to expect minority races to do any better in this matter than the rest of us, we may be sure that in the long run, given the opportunity, they will do at least as well.

The democratic solution to racial problems can be found in one way only: by full participation of minority groups in the whole community. We, the majority, will never agree as to exactly the steps that must be taken in housing, recreation, education, and business opportunities for minority races. There is, however, one sixty-four-dollar decision that we are obligated once and for all to make. Do they fully participate in making all the other secondary decisions or do they not? The alternatives of the nonparticipation of racial minorities in the progressive solution of their own problems is quite unthinkable in Pasadena, U.S.A., in 1948.

The chief reason for the existence of the Pasadena Interracial Commission and its claim on you for interest, support, and attention is its democratic process (representatives of all racial groups meeting together on equal footing, working together on racial problems), which is even more important than any specific steps it recommends or brings to pass.

But if the community as a whole neglects the commission and frustrates its attempts to move forward toward its goal, the commission tends to become an unfair safety valve for some of us to let off steam and will at the last become worse than useless.

But if, on the other hand, the Pasadena Interracial Commission leads to the development of trusted leaders of minority races and to democratically improved conditions for racial minorities and finally to such participation by the racial minorities in the total community of Pasadena so that at last it itself is no longer necessary, then all the efforts of its members will have then been infinitely worthwhile.

Chapter 8

LAW AND ORDER AND
CHRISTIAN DUTY *

THE United Presbyterian Church is a church of law and order. The standard and authority for what Presbyterians believe and for their moral duty is the Bible, consisting of the Old and New Testaments as they witness to Jesus Christ, the very Word to Man from God. Our Confession of Faith tells Presbyterians that it is not only their civic duty, but also their Christian duty, to honor civil law and the civic magistrate.

> It is the duty of people to pray for Magistrates, to honor their persons, to pay them tribute and other dues, to obey their lawful commands, and to be subject to their authority for conscience sake (C. XXXIII, 4).

From this you can see why I feel it important to preach to you about "Law and Order and Christian Duty," since this is my first sermon since I was arrested just outside Baltimore, Maryland, for having, with others—ministers and laymen, Negro and white—broken deliberately the trespass law of that state. The occasion was a demonstration organized by the Congress of Racial Equality (CORE) designed to protest the standing indignity offered the large Negro community by a private amusement park which regularly advertises that it is open to the public (it even appears in Rand McNally maps) and just as regularly has refused admittance to all dark-skinned Negroes.

One of the most distinguished Presbyterians of Baltimore, Mr. Furman Templeton, an elder, the director of Baltimore's Urban

---

* On July 4, 1963, Dr. Blake was among a group of demonstrators arrested for attempting to integrate a Baltimore, Maryland, amusement park. The following sermon was preached shortly afterward in the First Presbyterian Church, New Canaan, Connecticut, on the text: "But Peter and the apostles answered, 'We must obey God rather than men'" (Acts 5:29).

League, was with me. He is a Negro. We approached the gate of the amusement park together. The guard stopped us, saying that we could not enter. I protested. The guard said that I could go in but Mr. Templeton could not. I protested again. The trespass law (in digest form) was read to us. We were asked to leave the private property. We refused, continued our protest, and were arrested. Scores of others were arrested too, including six Roman Catholic priests, a Jewish rabbi, a dozen Protestant ministers, and many young people of both races. I was there as acting chairman of the Commission on Religion and Race of the National Council of Churches. Three others went with me from New York, representing the National Council of Churches, including Bishop Daniel Corrigan of the Protestant Episcopal Church. The question is: Is this kind of action right, or is it wrong? The fact that the demonstration was successful, that the owners of the park have promised to stop their discrimination this month, and that the charges against all of us have been dropped is not really relevant to my question. When, if ever, is it right to break the law? That is the question that I want you to think about with me this morning.

First, let me make it perfectly clear that breaking law is not something to be done lightly. Anarchy is a terrible thing. Disorder makes civilization impossible. I have already noted that Presbyterians have the tradition of honoring law, both civil and ecclesiastic. Anyone who has lived through a riot or revolution knows how much all of us ought to appreciate civil order and the police who enforce it for us all.

But let us be entirely clear that law is not God. It has always from the first been a basic Christian conviction that there are times when a Christian ought to break law. Let us look at a New Testament precedent. Peter and some of his fellow apostles had been officially ordered not to preach publicly that Jesus, the Christ, had been raised from the dead. They were in and out of jail several times, refusing to obey the injunction established by the Church and State officials (high priest, council, and senate). As Christians, Peter and the apostles believed that they must not obey any order, however legal, which would stop them from making their witness to the Lord Jesus Christ. They said, "We must obey God rather than men."

I do not believe that any of you would argue in general that it is never right to break a law. What about Christians or Jews under Hitler? What about the Boston Tea Party? What about the whole series of arrests in the New Testament when Christians regularly refused to obey some laws even when they were taught through the Apostle Paul that "the powers that be are ordained of God"?

But has the present-day effort by American Negroes to win equality *now* in voting, in education, in job opportunities and advancement, in housing, and in public facilities—even amusement parks—anything to do with witnessing to Jesus Christ, as in the first century?

It is quite clear that all of the highest authorities in the Church of Jesus Christ do so believe. Our own General Assembly has repeatedly made it clear that the white man's treatment of the Negro in our free nation is morally wrong and that our normal treatment of the Negro even in the Church itself is morally wrong and a betrayal of Christ. The Pope has made it clear that this is also the Roman Catholic understanding. The presiding bishop of the Protestant Episcopal Church spoke most eloquently and officially this spring in the same vein. So all the major churches in the whole world!

The World Council of Churches has been willing to lose from its membership several South African churches rather than weaken its witness to the Christian importance of racial equality and justice.

The general board of the National Council of Churches, in the same way as our own General Assembly, has asked us all to begin now to act in harmony with our Christian profession. But why just now? Why do we act now, apparently encouraging an increasing lawlessness on the part of the Negro community? It is clear enough that we should have begun to witness our convictions in this matter much sooner, but there are at least two reasons why I plead with each of you today to consider what may be your Christian duty in this battle for justice and equality in 1963 in the U.S.A.

First, the nation faces a crisis. It is not a sectional crisis; it is a national crisis. For one hundred years, since its fathers were freed from chattel slavery, the Negro community has on the whole followed Christian nonviolent leadership in trying to win a place of dignity and equality according to our American Constitution.

In some states Negroes do not yet have the right to vote, either because of intimidation or unjust local laws. Due to interrelated discrimination in getting jobs, finding housing, and good opportunities for education, most Negroes find it almost impossible to move out of the lowest social and economic strata of our society. It was not too long ago in California that we had in my town Negro college graduates operating garbage trucks because they were discriminated against in jobs for which they were prepared at great effort and sacrifice. Is it then surprising that many other Negroes drop out of high school when they see how hard it is to get ahead, even if you are good? Is it surprising that there are not enough Negroes ready for good jobs when some do open up? Then why are we surprised that Negroes generally are forced into crowded housing—high priced—because they do not qualify for other communities as "our kind of people."

I say these inequalities are all interrelated; a push toward solving them all together, along with the right to vote everywhere and the right to public accommodation everywhere, is the only solution. And the people who are preventing this national and Christian solution are not the Governor Faubuses and the Governor Wallaces away off in Arkansas or Alabama. The responsible people for the stalemate in August, 1963, are we white Christians who have isolated our bodies from the realities of the city by living in the suburbs and our minds from the realities of the injustice our laws and social patterns impose upon Negroes by forgetting all about them whenever they become quiet and patient. We have a national crisis which may lead to all sorts of violence and even revolution if we do not now decide to throw our persons and our influence into changing the segregated pattern of American life. For the Negro community is tired of being patient under a century of excessively slow progress. They have seen what less qualified peoples of their own race have done in Africa to become free, and they don't intend to wait any longer. If there is increasing violence in the United States, it will not be the fault of Negroes striving for fairness and justice. It will be the fault of all of us who, in apathy and ignorance, let injustice continue. I might say here that if any of you are worried at the lack of popularity of our American way of life in Asia, Africa, and even in Europe, you could do more to make "the free world" strong by helping establish justice and dignity in our land for the colored people in it than in any other way I know. Communism makes worldwide progress with each headline of violence in Alabama, Mississippi, New York, or Illinois.

But that is merely the national crisis. The second reason why you and I must act now in 1963 to establish justice—and this second reason is of first importance for any Christian—is that there is an equally grave crisis in the Christian Church. A part of the crisis we face in the Church is that Negro Christians have now largely lost their faith in the sincerity of the professions of white Christians in the matter of race. If we do not act the way we have talked, the Negro community will turn increasingly from the Christian Church to which up until now Negroes have been amazingly loyal.

But there is a greater crisis yet in the Church. It would be my conservative estimate that there are at least five thousand Presbyterian pastors who have a bad conscience about what they are doing to help right Negro wrongs. And this is because they are fearful that you would not support them if they simply obeyed the gospel and led their congregations to take the lead in this contest for human dignity for all men for whom Christ died. I estimate that five thousand Presbyterian ministers hesitate to lead in this effort because they are afraid of their jobs. And they have good reason. Again and again congregations all over this land have made it clear that they do not want their pastors to be "controversial," even when that controversial position is clearly based upon the gospel of Jesus Christ.

This leads us to a further crisis in the ministry of our Church. I am sure you know that the recruitment of the ablest young men for the pastorate has fallen off in recent years. I am sure that one of the chief reasons why the ablest of our dedicated young men do not look forward with joy and enthusiasm to becoming pastors is that they do not want ever to find themselves in the embarrassing position in which too many sincere and conscientious pastors are today. Despite all the attractiveness of the pastorate and its daily opportunity to serve Jesus Christ, these young men do not see congregations willing to follow truly Christian leadership.

I dare not estimate how many of the three and a quarter million United Persbyterian members like you have bad consciences too. You know that we all have allowed our own comfort, our own prosperity, our own fears, and our own conscious and unconscious prejudices to guide us in our actions—and equally in our lack of actions—rather than our professed Christian faith.

Frankly, the Christian Church in America does not look much like a Christian Church as far as race is concerned. We look like a religious club for our own kind of people, the religious holy embroidery on a secular culture which is essentially more and more selfish and fearful the wealthier and more comfortable we become. I say then that the reason people like you and me should stand with our Negro brethren in their effort to achieve equality is that if we do not we shall reveal ourselves at last as hypocritical and we shall fail in our day to witness to Jesus Christ whom we proclaim to be the Savior of the world.

One of my correspondents since July 4 wrote me to inquire if I thought Jesus Christ would ever demonstrate and cause violence. I wrote him that that was entirely too simple a way to put the question. I am sure that the white and Negro school kids who have gathered in churches all over the South and then gone out to sit in physical danger in protests at lunch counters are nearer to the Kingdom than most of us.

What then can you do? May I conclude by suggesting some very concrete actions:

1. You can try to get Congress to pass stronger civil rights legislation. If you believe in *upholding the law*, will you not do your part to get the laws in this matter strengthened? Write your two senators and your congressman today. Tell them that you believe civil rights to be a moral matter, that you want good legislation passed this summer, and that you do not want your representatives to make this a partisan issue nor will you countenance their allowing a filibuster to prevent this needed legislation. This effort will cost you fifteen cents and an hour's time to write good letters.

And come and meet me and thousands of others in Washington, D.C., on August 28, where there is to be the greatest orderly demonstration of concern that the capital has ever seen. The invitation is to you. Unless people like you begin to demonstrate it is now freely predicted that no civil rights legislation will pass, and if the Congress is unable or unwilling to legislate, it is freely predicted that a new and more violent phase in civil rights demonstrations will then begin.

2. Tomorrow join the National Association for the Advance-

ment of Colored People and make a whopping big contribution to its legal and defense fund. Again let me appeal here to any of you who really would uphold the law. For the N.A.A.C.P. has, for a quarter of a century and more, pressed in court after court trying to honor the law by seeking justice and equality for all under the Constitution.

On Tuesday join the Urban League, a national organization that has been working for years to make a break for Negroes in getting jobs and being advanced according to merit. Make a contribution to the Urban League and add to your charities (all, by the way, are not deductible) the Southern Leadership Conference of Martin Luther King, the Congress of Racial Equality, headed by James L. Farmer, the Student Non-violent Coordinating Committee. These are the organizations that are leading this effort for justice and equality now. If you are unwilling to give to them, give then to the National Council of Churches or to your own United Presbyterian Church and earmark the funds for their commissions on religion and race.

What else can you do besides writing letters and joining organizations and supporting them?

3. You can make it your project where you work to see that jobs are open to Negroes who are qualified and that your business will train unqualified Negroes the same way you train and upgrade presently unqualified white people. If you don't work, but are a stockholder, write the management and tell management or owner that you want your company to be leaders in enlightened employment policies as to race. You may lose a bit of your popularity if you really take this seriously, but you must begin where you have influence.

4. You can pray each night for the Negro community and its leaders; you can pray for the people who are in Mississippi jails under excessive bond and have been there for weeks and months. You can pray for any of us who day by day have to make hard decisions, realizing that we may be wrong in them but must nevertheless try to make them as Christians.

5. You can begin an effort to make it possible for anybody who has the money to buy and rent in your town. I know I am moving into a touchy subject here. I do not speak only to you. I speak to myself as a resident of this lovely spot of isolation and retreat. Ah, but this is the place that you have found for your own family's

peace and development. "Don't make us ruin our hometown!" But suburban living by the power structure of our society is one of the causes of the racial crisis. I have driven off and on from New York to this area of Connecticut for thirty years. I noticed that recent racial disturbances on the Boston Post Road in the Bronx are in a part of the city I used to drive through. But I have not been on that road for twenty years. We have thruways and expressways now which make it possible to isolate ourselves almost completely from any ugliness. And in these twenty years more and more Americans are driven from rural to urban life, and all those who are poor live in increasingly crowded cities. You will find that you will not increase your popularity in your town if you really mean to back the housing program already begun by the churches of New Canaan.

6. You can protest every time you hear anyone blaming Negroes for agitation or saying they ask too much. Some do ask too much and some ask for the wrong things. But the cause of extremism is justice delayed and we, not they, are responsible for that.

What you can do is to begin to act your faith even if it may lead you to arrest, ridicule, or poverty, or even physical danger. The widely publicized July 4 demonstration in Maryland will not be important unless it symbolizes and encourages the members of our churches to act in a new pattern of witness to Jesus Christ with regard to racial equality and justice. If this happens widely, not only among a few ministers and members, it will go far to mark the very renewal of our Church by the Holy Spirit of God in faith and in hope and in love. It is time for us all to stand up and be counted.

"We must obey God rather than men," said Peter and the apostles, and that simple decision became the foundation of the Church of Jesus Christ and the reason for its winning the world to him. It is not easy always to know how to obey God. But no one who is failing to try to find the way to change the racially segregated pattern of American life can claim these days to be trying very hard to obey God. And then when we have done our best we will still be sinners, as the gospel reminds us, and we will need each other's fellowship and prayers, as sinners who are for-given freely when they do repent of evil and turn to God through Jesus Christ. For the Christian gospel is a power for reconciliation of sinners to God, and of all men to all men. In worship here or in any Christian sanctuary we need to be helped to be agents of that Divine reconciliation, loving one another even when we deeply disagree, loving the enemies we make and those, too, who make us their enemies. Thus the Church of Jesus Christ will be His Church. Thus will the Church witness to its Lord.

Chapter 9

LATE WE COME *

I WISH indeed that I were able to speak for all Protestant, Anglican, and Orthodox Christians as I speak in behalf of full justice and freedom for all born or living under the American flag. But that is precisely the point. If all the members and all the ministers of the constituency I represent here today were indeed ready to stand and march with you for jobs and freedom for the Negro people, together with all the Roman Catholic Church and all of the synagogues in America, the battle for full civil rights and dignity would already be won.

I do, in fact, officially represent the Commission on Religion and Race of the National Council of Churches. And I am honored to be here in the highest tradition of that Council and of the churches which constitute it, thus to represent one of the sponsoring bodies of this March for Jobs and Freedom.

For many years now, the National Council of Churches and most of its constituent communions have said all the right things about civil rights. Our official pronouncements for years have clearly called for "a nonsegregated church in a nonsegregated society." But as of August 28, 1963, we have achieved neither a nonsegregated church nor a nonsegregated society. And it is partly because the churches of America have failed to put their own house in order that 100 years after the Emancipation Proclamation, 175 years after the adoption of the Constitution, and 173 years after the adoption of the Bill of Rights, the United States of America still faces a racial crisis.

---

* The following address was delivered at the Lincoln Memorial in Washington, D.C., August 28, 1963, on the occasion of the March on Washington for Jobs and Freedom. Dr. Blake was a cochairman of the civil rights demonstration.

We do not, therefore, come to this Lincoln Memorial today in any arrogant spirit of moral or spiritual superiority to "set the nation straight" or to judge or denounce the American people in whole or in part. Rather we come—late, late we come—in the reconciling and repentant spirit in which the humble Lincoln of Illinois once replied to a delegation of morally arrogant churchmen, "Never say God is on our side, rather pray that we may be found on God's side."

We come in the fear of God that moved Thomas Jefferson of Virginia, whose memorial stands there across the lagoon, once to say: "Indeed, I tremble for my country, when I reflect that God is just."

Yes, we come to march behind and with those amazingly able leaders of the Negro Americans who, to the shame of almost every white American, have alone and without us mirrored the suffering of the Cross of Jesus Christ; they have offered their bodies to arrest and to violence, to the hurt and indignity of fire hoses and dogs, of derision and of poverty, and some to death for this just cause. We come—late we come—but we come to present ourselves, our souls and bodies, to be "a living sacrifice, holy and acceptable to God, which is our reasonable service," in a kind of tangible and visible sacrament which alone in times like these can manifest to a troubled world the grace available at communion table or high altar.

We come in prayer that we, in our time, may be more worthy to bear the name our tongues so fluently profess. We come in faith that the God who made us and gave His Son for us and for our salvation will overrule the fears and hatreds that so far have prevented the establishment of full racial justice in our beloved country. We come in hope that those who have marched today are but a token of a new and massive high determination of all men of religion and patriotism to win in this "nation under God . . . liberty and justice for all." We come in that love revealed in Jesus Christ, which reconciles into true community all men of every color, race, and nation who respond in faith and obedience to Him.

Chapter 10

SOUTH AFRICA IS A PART
OF AFRICA*

AFRICA is a large continent and it is almost as difficult to gener-
alize about it as it is to write about Europe in general—as if
Europe were not divided politically, culturally, and economically.
As Americans turn much more of their attention toward Africa
these days, the most important word that must be said is: Don't
suppose that you know enough about the complexities of present-
day Africa to have a specific judgment about the wise or Christian
next step in Tanganyika, Kenya, or Nyasaland merely on the
ground that a wave of nationalism and a thirst for independence
are general among all black Africans.

I mention the three areas above as important areas about
which I do not know enough firsthand to write about, since my
recent visit was confined to the Union of South Africa and to
several parts of West Africa only.

Let me list some differences among the areas which I did visit,
to make clear some contrasts. In Nigeria, Cameroun (formerly
French), in Rio Muni and Fernando Po (formerly Spanish Guinea,
now integral provinces of Spain), and in Belgian Congo, the
white settlers and landowners are comparatively few in number.
In South Africa, in contrast, there are three million whites of
Dutch and British descent with all of the former and many of the
latter as much African as any people on the continent, since they
have now no other homeland. The French in the Cameroun and
the British in Nigeria have adjusted relatively easily to African
demands for self-rule, since the white settlers can be resettled
elsewhere, if the necessity should arise. Furthermore, in both these
areas there is an educated class of Africans who clearly can rule

* The following article was written following a visit to South Africa in 1959.

their countries in today's circumstances better than the European rulers they are replacing in more or less orderly fashion.

In Belgian Congo, Spanish Guinea, and the large Portuguese territories, however, there is not by any means enough educated leadership to take over self-rule without probable chaos. Thus the immediate future looks good economically in Nigeria and Cameroun (capital is ready and waiting to be invested), whereas white owners are willing to sell property at sacrifice in Belgian Congo and there are no buyers. The Iberian governments are resisting (so far successfully) political moves for independence in their territories; and, despite the general wave of nationalism among black Africans, these territories do not yet show enough unrest to discourage European economic activity in the limited old-style colonial pattern. Most large investments have been made on the expectation of a 20 percent per year profit; thus five to ten years is as far ahead as it is usually necessary to look.

South Africa is clearly unique, not because it is simply different from the rest of Africa, but because it is different in a most complex way. Let us look at a few facts, withholding judgments until those facts are clearly before us.

The Union of South Africa comprises a territory of 472,500 square miles (twice the size of France, five times the size of the United Kingdom). In 1956 the population figures were: whites nearly three million; full-blooded Africans (Bantu, as the whites prefer to call them, since the whites are African as well) nearly ten million; Coloured (mixed races not unlike our own Negro population) nearly one and one-half million; and Asiatics (Indian and Malay) nearly one-half million. These people are, of course, not evenly spread over the nation. For example, nearly all the Coloureds are in the Cape Province, making the racial situation in that part roughly one million whites, a little over a million Coloured, and two and three-quarter million Africans (Bantu), with less than 100,000 Asiatics. In contrast, Natal, a much smaller area and more heavily British in culture, has 300,000 whites, 800,000 Asiatics (mostly Indian) with nearly two million Africans (Bantu) and less than 100,000 Coloureds.

These contrasts in population, even within the Union, produce different problems and different attitudes toward the problems among the various racial and cultural groups. It is important to note that the whites (or Europeans) have been settled for about the same length of time as we have been settled in North America. (The Dutch arrived at the Cape in 1652.) The Europeans are divided into two cultural groups, divided by language (English and Afrikaans), by history (the Boer War), by economics (the British wealthier entrepreneurs in the cities and the Afrikaners, until the depression of the thirties, almost all in rural areas), by attitude toward the homeland (British South Africans of several generations standing are apt to call Britain home, while Afrikaners are culturally almost entirely emancipated from Dutch connections), by political party (the British support the United Party, which is a party of typical British compromise, while Afrikaners generally support the Nationalist Party, best known abroad for its racial policy of apartheid), and by religion. The British are Anglican, Methodist, Presbyterian, Congregationalist, and Baptist, with a large secular orientation, while Afrikaners are almost all members of the Reformed Church and much less influenced by modern secular culture.

Even the above analysis of differences is quite inadequate. There are for example many Europeans who are bilingual and are descended from both British and Dutch, not to mention French Huguenots, etc. Most Afrikaners understand English and many speak it fluently. Much fewer of the English are in any full sense bilingual.

Furthermore, it is a mistake to think of the large Dutch Reformed Church as being merely the African counterpart of the Church in the Netherlands. The largest of the Reformed Churches is an African Church (not racially black, but African in the sense that the Protestant Episcopal Church and the Presbyterian Churches in this country are American and not British). This largest Reformed Church looks back to such figures as Andrew Murray, who came out from Scotland as a spiritual progenitor. It is a South African church.

To understand the racial problem of South Africa, it is vital to know something of the above analysis, especially since the Nationalist Party, now in power, is committed to a strict policy of apartheid—that is, to provide for the separate development of each of the four racial groupings of the population, European, African (Bantu), Coloured, and Asiatic. Americans naturally have a good deal of skepticism about the possibility of the working out of any "separate but equal" racial policy. Nothing I saw in

South Africa made me any less skeptical of this than I was before I made my trip. But I do think it is important for us to understand the white South African, especially the serious-minded Dutch Reformed Church man and his attitude toward the racial problem.

In the first place, we should note that he is no more prejudiced than many a white man in our own country. In fact, I noticed less personal prejudice than one might expect to find among white people of our own Southern states. Eating with people of color under Church auspices presented no problem anywhere I visited. Furthermore, the Afrikaner (except in some extreme fundamentalist strongholds) does not try to use the Bible to justify racial discrimination. The resolutions adopted by the Synods of the Dutch Reformed Church make this entirely evident. There are, however, several positions that leaders and members of the Dutch Reformed Church typically take which, unless modified from within the life of the Church itself, promise continued criticism from abroad and, I fear, ultimate disaster.

1. They take as given the government's policy of apartheid. This is not, however, universally true even in the Dutch Reformed Church. I met a number of ministers who were critical of various aspects of the Nationalist government's racial policy, but I came away with the impression that few would vote against it and that most accept the main lines of government policy as something that cannot be changed.

2. They take as given the economic necessity of migratory black African labor, on account of which African men are away from their homes and families for long stretches of time with all sorts of evil social consequences. (It used to be that the contract labor of the gold and diamond mines was the dark side of the labor picture, but now the worst part of the picture is the less regulated but general and massive use of cheap and primitive African manpower from the Reserves for all sorts of industrial purposes in increasingly urban South Africa.)

3. They accept as a right and basic motivation for political action the preservation of "our Christian way of life."

4. They accept the white man's cultural superiority as reason or excuse for excluding all others, however well educated, from the right to vote. They therefore tend to disregard as irrelevant the political aspirations of the Africans (Bantu) and even of the Coloureds, since it seems obvious to them that the vote by the

overwhelming numbers of non-Europeans would not only wipe out white civilization, but bring nothing but tragedy to the dark-skinned people as well.

5. As a transition to civilization for the Africans on the Reserves, they seem to be committed to a revival of primitive tribal customs, which anthropologists know cannot be revived since they were dependent on an isolation and an economy that no longer exist.

These five blind spots in what seemed to me to be the typical moderate Afrikaner position make it unlikely that others outside will be fair and appreciative of the good things the Nationalists and the Dutch Reformed Church are doing. The extensive slum clearance and housing program in the major cities, the increasing missionary programs, including evangelism, health services, and education, the criticism of the government for specific hardships and injustices caused by apartheid, and even the theoretical realization that apartheid is only a stage in the development of a multiracial society—all these good things, and a great deal of Christian good will and concern, are obscured and likely will be rendered useless by the five blind spots listed above.

This analysis leads me to make a few suggestions as to our own attitude toward South Africa and especially toward the Dutch Reformed Church, its leaders, and members. These suggestions are made not only to white American Christians but also to Negro American Christians who will undoubtedly have more influence on the African continent in the next decades than any of us whose skins are white.

1. Let us recognize and emphasize every good and Christian motivation that exists among the leaders and members of the Dutch Reformed Church in South Africa. These fellow Christians need to be loved and understood more than they need to be criticized and hated. They are troubled and they are sincerely disturbed at what they feel is a worldwide misunderstanding of them and their position.

2. While giving full credit for the Anglican and other English-speaking churches' minority witness against apartheid by deed and word, let us not suppose that the differences between these churches are due entirely to an ethical or theological superiority. I found as much desire for true Christian understanding and witness among the Dutch Reformed as I did among the other churches in South Africa.

3. Let us seek to involve South African Christians of all races as fully as possible in the Ecumenical Movement and in its councils, in the hope and faith that it is this process which will be most helpful both to South Africa and to the Ecumenical Movement.

4. Let us all remember that our own Christianity is too much conditioned by our own theological, social, and political history and bias; let us not spoil by arrogance such witness as we make.

5. And finally, let us remember that it is an unreal and unchristian social prejudice to suppose that all black Africans are and will be any more virtuous than white Africans or any less subject to racial prejudice or to extreme nationalism when they have succeeded in winning self-rule and independence. For even then the Christian Church is apt to be as much embarrassed as it is today when it contemplates the gulf between its members' Christian professions and their political and economic actions.

Chapter 11

PEACE *

WE address this message to you at this time because of our deep concern that Christians in the United States are failing thus far to make their specific contribution to the maintenance of peace in the world, having been almost silent while our nation's involvement in Vietnam increases step by step.

Many voices are being heard: that of the Administration, justifying each step of escalation as a rational and logical necessity of our long-time policy of the containment of communism; radical voices in the university community and elsewhere calling for withdrawal from Southeast Asia and even sometimes for a victory for the Vietcong and North Vietnam; radically conservative and militaristic voices pressing the government to unleash our bombers with their overwhelming power to blast Hanoi and even the People's Republic of China if necessary, their appeal becoming more palatable with the release of each casualty list of young Americans.

More and more the mass media begin to reflect a psychology of inevitable war, so that every criticism of United States policy from any quarter is made to sound like treason on the ground that it gives aid and comfort to the enemy.

The reason Christians have a specific responsibility to speak and to criticize is that they have a loyalty to God which must transcend every other loyalty, and they belong to one family with all other Christians on all six continents. At the same time they seek to be loyal citizens of their nation.

We of the General Board support the government and Admin-

———

* The following Message to Churches was drafted by Dr. Blake and adopted with some amendments on December 3, 1965, as an official statement of the General Board of the National Council of Churches.

istration, especially in the following aspects of its policy in Vietnam:

1. So far, it has been a restrained policy even though great pressure has had to be resisted against the escalation into an all-out war.

2. We believe in the integrity of the administration as it has expressed publicly its willingness to negotiate unconditionally to find peace in Vietnam.

3. We support its willingness to give major leadership in financing with other nations massive economic and social development for the peoples in the Mekong Valley, whether friendly or hostile to us today.

We have just passed a new policy statement on Vietnam which we believe deals intelligently and in Christian understanding with the complex issues which face our nation there. We have commended this to you for study, but we must do more.

As Christian members of a worldwide Christian family we must remind ourselves and our government of these convictions:

1. We believe that war in this nuclear age settles hardly anything and may destroy everything.

2. We believe that unilateral action by the United States in Southeast Asia will not lead to peace. We must seek with new determination to unite our efforts through the United Nations and its concerned members.

3. We believe that if the United States follows a unilateral policy in Vietnam, no conceivable victory there can compensate for the distrust and hatred of the United States that is being generated each day throughout much of the world because we are seen as a predominantly white nation using our overwhelming military strength to kill more and more Asians.

4. We believe that the loss of life and the indescribable sufferings of the civilian population of South Vietnam over a period of more than twenty years of conflict and the increasing number of casualties in the armed forces, together with the suffering accompanying this increasing loss of life, should be such a matter of Christian conscience and concern that Church members should give strong support to efforts to care for the people involved and to end the war as quickly as possible.

In view of these convictions we call upon Christians in the United States to do three things:

1. The first thing we must do, and perhaps the most difficult and most important, is to maintain our spiritual and ethical sensitivity and keep before us our awareness of the imperatives of the Christian gospel. In wartime this is often the first casualty. These imperatives we all know, for they are clearly written in the New Testament. "Love your enemies and pray for those who persecute you. . . . If your enemy is hungry, feed him. . . . And he made from one every nation of men to live on all the face of the earth. . . . Do not be conformed to this world but be transformed by the renewal of your mind. . . . Do not be overcome by evil, but overcome evil with good."

2. Let peacemaking be the priority of our Christian witness so that we may be truly children of God in these difficult times.

3. Support the efforts of the National Council of Churches in an approach to the World Council of Churches and Pope Paul VI in a common attempt to mobilize the worldwide Christian community in support of a just alternative to war.

The General Board of the National Council of Churches adopts the above message and directs that it be made widely available to the members of all of our constituent churches.

It further directs the officers of the National Council of Churches to take the initiative in seeking through the World Council of Churches in cooperation with the Roman Catholic Church to mobilize the worldwide Christian community to develop and support a just alternative to war.

Chapter 12

AMERICAN LIBERTY AND
THE CHURCHES*

Dr. Blake. Senator Hennings, Senator O'Mahoney, ladies and gentlemen, my name is Eugene Carson Blake, of Philadelphia, Pennsylvania. I am a minister of the Presbyterian Church of the United States of America and presently president of the National Council of the Churches of Christ in America.

It seems to me that it is entirely appropriate that there be asked on this occasion at least one churchman citizen to speak on this Constitution Day before this particular subcommittee of the Senate.

Historically the churches of our country have been vitally concerned with religious liberty and with all our liberties. Today the churches have as great a stake in human liberty as they had when the Bill of Rights was adopted.

Our history makes it clear that one of the very important streams flowing into the river of American liberty is that religious one which springs up out of the soul of a man in the presence of his God.

When, at the end of the eighteenth century, our forefathers were creating the political instruments of American freedom, many of their most creative ideas had come down to them from ancestors who had fled their homes in the Continent of Europe or the British Isles as their only way of escape from religious persecution. Before their forced emigration these men had had their fill of penalties imposed upon them by government for their opinions and beliefs. They were tired of being ignored or even punished

---

* The following testimony was given September 17, 1955—during the McCarthy era—to the Subcommittee on Constitutional Rights of the Senate Committee on the Judiciary.

for having had the effrontery to petition a hostile government for the redress of their grievances.

Modern ideas of tolerance were not widespread anywhere in the eighteenth century, but it is clear that as the United States was being founded, men of very deep religious conviction joined equally with more secular-minded people in an endeavor to find a way to set up a government strong enough to resist anarchy, which gives way always to tyranny, and yet not so strong as to become tyrannic itself. This was and is the problem of liberty, how to create a government able to protect the liberties of all its citizens from one another, and at the same time unable to usurp their liberties itself.

A new idea grew out of the unique combination of religious conviction and the then "modern enlightenment." It was the acceptance by both churchmen and other citizens of the concept of limited sovereignty. During the Middle Ages in Europe the struggle had long continued between Church and State, as to which ultimately should control the destinies of men and nations. The struggle seesawed between Canossa and Avignon. The theory of the ultimate and absolute sovereignty of the Church was countered at last with the theory of the divine rights of kings.

It was clear that the American Revolutionists could not accept the divine right of George III of Great Britain, and too many of them had had experience of being a religious minority in an ecclesiastically dominated state to be willing to chance any religious establishment.

And so it happened that both the American State and the American churches accepted the idea that both were under the authority of the same Sovereign Creator of all men and nations.

As a churchman, may I say that it is my belief that for the liberty of men and for the prosperity of religion it is equally as important for churches to recognize their human limitations as it is for civil governments to recognize theirs.

Besides the sovereignty of God there was another important religious idea that was set into the framework of American liberty. It was the doctrine of sin—I dare say it—of the depravity of man.

If the most "advanced" political ideas current at the end of the eighteenth century had been the only influence that had framed the American Constitution, I am afraid that with a much more logical and efficient government we would not have had our liberties quite so well protected as they have been. Because they took seriously the doctrine of human depravity, the religious founders of our nation made it certain that powers were so balanced in their new government that no absolute and corrupting power could find its way into the hands of an individual or even a large group of individuals without there appearing a counterweight sufficient to preserve the liberties of the people from any tyrannic minority or even from a tyrannic majority.

It was thus out of a unique combination of religious conviction and "modern enlightenment" that the American tradition of Church and State was formed. And I am, therefore, happy to express to you, as a churchman citizen, some of the concerns shared by many churches in the area covered by the Bill of Rights.

Please note that I said "many churches." No one could speak equally for all churches and say such a thing.

I do not want to make a long or exhaustive list of grievances.

First, let me underline the chief concern. Let no government or branch thereof think of itself as the arbiter or controller of men's opinions, convictions, or faiths. No free man will allow his convictions—religious, economic, or political—to be controlled by the State.

Let government remain the servant of the American people, not their master. Let no part of government forget that it, along with the churches and the people, is subject to the judgment and justice of Almighty God. Let us even in the most trying of circumstances exemplify the humility of Abraham Lincoln, who, in the Civil War, was not so bold as ever to identify the cause of the Union with the will of God.

And I speak as a Yankee whose two grandfathers were captains in the Grand Army of the Republic.

In recent years there has been a committee of the House of Representatives on Un-American Activities.

And I use as an illustration the committee of the House, although other committees in the legislative halls of states and government could be used.

Although I do not presume to assess the value of this committee in the development of information needed by the Congress for legislation against subversive threats to our country, I am compelled to say that many of the side effects of this committee's activities have caused most churches grave concern. Let me list the reasons for this concern.

First, the very name of the committee raises a question. For there has been a growing tendency on the part of our representatives in government to suppose that it is within the competence of the State to determine what is and what is not American.

But from the beginning the glory of the American way of life has been the encouragement of diversity of conscientious opinion and conviction, and American law is concerned with overt, illegal actions only.

Second, the committee has used techniques in hearings which have in effect turned the witness into one accused and has not afforded many a witness an opportunity or the means to protect himself and his reputation, means which even a legally indicted citizen is afforded in any court.

Third, the committee has failed to distinguish between allegations of disloyalty and proved disloyalty.

Fourth, unsupported allegations, which could have been easily proven false, have on occasions been disseminated on the committee's letterhead to the hurt of the reputation of loyal Americans.

Fifth, the committee has been itself confused as to the difference between disloyalty to our country and the holding of opinions which happen to be politically unpopular or publicly embarrassing.

Sixth, the committee has on occasion lost all historical perspective, implying disloyalty for past associations of some citizens, which associations at the time when they occurred were shared by other citizens whose loyalty it would not dare to challenge.

I have used one committee of the Congress and its activities as an illustration of a kind of governmental action which is of grave concern to many of the churches.

Let me, in order to be entirely fair, take an illustration that causes some concern from each of the other branches of the federal government.

A proposal was made a few years ago by the Chief Executive of the nation that diplomatic relations should be established with the head of one of the Christian churches. All of the churches in the United States—except the one it was proposed to recognize, and it took no official position on the matter—were deeply concerned and made their concern vocal enough so that nothing came of the proposal.

Whether or not such diplomatic recognition can be fairly construed as contrary to the First Amendment may be a moot question. But that is not the point.

Such a recognition must be justified on the ground of one church having a preferred position in the world religious scene or on the ground that there were nonreligious reasons sufficient for it.

Most American churches would be against such a recognition on either ground, even if it were proposed that equally important diplomatic recognition be offered to their own churches. And this on the basis of the clause against establishment or preference of one religion or church as against another.

In the constitution of one of our American churches, which was first published in 1788, these words occur:

> That "God alone is Lord of the conscience; and hath left it free from the doctrine and commandments of men, which are in anything contrary to His word, or beside it in matters of faith or worship." Therefore they consider the rights of private judgment, in all matters that respect religions, as universal and unalienable: they do not even wish to see any religious constitution aided by the civil power, further than may be necessary for protection and security and, at the same time, be equal and common to all others.

I have used but one illustration from the executive branch, because it is of such basic concern to religious equality in the United States. There are many other problems in the executive branch, on which there would be more unanimity on the part of the churches as to abuses that threaten us all.

I merely mention the extraordinary power exercised by the Attorney General in establishing a list of subversive organizations, the control by a bureau of the issuance of passports to free citizens, and the injustice suffered by many loyal Americans because of inadequately safeguarded security procedures.

Finally, let me express one concern in the judicial realm.

I speak with great hesitation. The churches of this country have confidence in the Supreme Court that it will continue to interpret the Constitution in such a way as will protect the religious liberty of even unpopular and splinter minorities.

But in this process we must confess to a fear that in order to do this, the Court may tend to change this nation from a nation under God to a completely secular state in which the law is interpreted as creating a gulf between religion and government, which it was never intended should exist.

Most American Christians would prefer this error rather than the contrary one which would allow the State and its instruments to be used by churches for their ecclesiastical purposes.

In education, for example, American Christians believe in the primary responsibility of parents for the religious education of their own children. They believe in the right of churches or private individuals to set up schools of their own for these purposes, but most American Christians believe this right does not include governmental financial support for them.

But this ought not to mean that the public, tax-supported school must be irreligious or nonreligious or antireligious. The Constitution ought to protect the public schools equally from sectarianism and from secularism. This is not easy to do. Some decisions of the Supreme Court have come closer to the Church's ideal in this regard than others.

And it will be a continuing concern of the churches that the cause of faith shall not be set backward by the development of a tax-supported public school system whose values are determined by the State at a humanistic level rather than by the American people under the guidance of Almighty God.

Chapter 13

PRAYER IN PUBLIC SCHOOLS*

My name is Eugene Carson Blake. As Stated Clerk of the United Presbyterian Church in the United States of America, I am grateful for the privilege to address this committee in opposition to proposed amendments to the U.S. Constitution relating to school prayers, Bible reading, etc.

The First Amendment to our federal Constitution, a masterpiece of simplicity and conciseness, has stood for almost 175 years as a civil counterpart to this theological statement by my own ecclesiastical forebears. It begins:

> Congress shall make no law respecting an establishment of religion, or prohibiting the free exercise thereof. . . .

I would vigorously oppose any effort to change either my own Church's or the United States Constitution with respect to the implications of these two principles. They articulate, each in its own way, the inviolability of the citadel of a man's faith and worship, the freedom of his belief and practice, hewn out at so great a cost in the history of Western man.

Neither our ecclesiastical nor our civil forefathers foresaw precisely the mid-twentieth-century society that has developed in the United States, particularly with respect to our common public school system and the diversity of faiths represented among its teachers and pupils. Hence, in May of 1963, the 175th General Assembly of the United Presbyterian Church, meeting in Des Moines, Iowa, took two actions in harmony with that taken nearly two centuries ago, but addressed to our contemporary situation. One of them spoke implicitly, and the other explicitly, to the

---

* The following testimony was given April 29, 1964, before the Judiciary Committee of the House of Representatives.

matter now before this committee. I would point out that both
actions were taken *prior* to the U.S. Supreme Court's decision in
the Schempp and Murray cases involving prayer and Bible reading
as devotional acts in the public schools.

First, with respect to the practice of holding religious observ-
ances as a part of the program of public schools, the 175th General Assembly adopted the following position:

> . . . Religious observances [should] never be held in a public
> school or introduced into the public school system as a part of its
> program. Bible reading in connection with courses in the American
> heritage, world history, literature, the social sciences, and other
> academic subjects is completely appropriate to public school instruc-
> tion. Bible reading and prayers as devotional acts tend toward indoc-
> trination or meaningless ritual and should be omitted for both
> reasons. Ministers, priests, and rabbis should be free to speak in
> public schools, provided their speaking does not constitute religious
> indoctrination or their presence form a part of a religious
> observance.

This statement was probably the most controversial part of a
larger statement on "Relations Between Church and State,"
approved by the same General Assembly. The entire report, including the portion I have just quoted, was studied during the previous
year by 131 presbyteries and 989 congregational groups in our
denomination. The portion on prayer and Bible reading—the most
disputed part—was approved by vote in over two-thirds of these.
The vote by which the entire report was adopted by the General
Assembly was 528 in favor and 298 opposed.

I cite these figures to indicate a point that, in my opinion,
deserves special consideration by the committee. We are all aware
of the considerable body of sentiment expressed in this country
that suggests some kind of amendment to the U.S. Constitution
so as to modify the import of the First Article in the Bill of
Rights. I daresay that much of that opinion is expressed by sincere
and devout church members, some indeed by members of the
United Presbyterian Church. But my own experience, and that
of other church leaders with whom I have discussed this matter,
is uniformly that where there is careful study of the issues involved
in this matter—as against an initial and unconsidered emotional
reaction—a substantial body of thoughtful American and church-

member opinion sees the dangers inherent in the practice of devotions in the public schools.

The other action taken by the General Assembly last year bears more directly upon the immediate concern of this committee with respect to proposed amendments to the Constitution relating to school prayers, Bible reading, etc. The official statement adopted said in part:

The 175th General Assembly

Reminds the church that the development and practice of Christian worship is the inescapable obligation of the congregation and the family, and not of the public schools.

Warns the church of an all-too-human tendency to look to the state and its agencies for support in fulfilling the church's mission. Such a tendency on the American scene endangers true religion as well as civil liberties. Consequently, this General Assembly calls the church to renewed worship, study, work, and sacrifice to fulfill its mission as God's people in the world.

Mr. Chairman, the history of Western civilization has examples in it—enough to give us pause—of countries that have shifted from one "religion" to another and back again as the prevailing forces of the government have caused a change in policy. The First Amendment, by removing the coercive forces of government from among those that play upon the theological convictions of the people, has served well to protect the freedom of belief of Americans. Any efforts, therefore, to tamper with this constitutional protection ought to cause us to pause and call into question those impulses that seem at first glance most congenial in attempting to enlist the power of government to strengthen the forces of faith. The forces that prevail tomorrow or next year or next generation may not be so congenial to our faith. As James Madison said in his great "Memorial and Remonstrance" in 1785:

Who does not see that the same authority which can establish Christianity, in exclusion of all other religions, may establish, with the same ease, any particular sect of Christians in exclusion of all other sects . . . ?

With no disturbance of his argument one could amend Mr. Madison's statement by substituting "theism" for Christianity and "other faith or no faith" for "any particular sect of Christians" so that the argument would run: Who does not see that the same authority which can establish theism in exclusion of all other religions may establish, with the same ease, other faith or no faith . . . ?

Mr. Chairman, I "take alarm" at this "experiment on our liberties," and urge the committee to oppose any change in the protections offered by the First Amendment. The Bill of Rights should remain unamended, for the rights are inalienable.

Chapter 14

SHOULD CHURCH PROPERTY BE TAXED?*

As a churchman, I know that churches have grown and prospered in the United States partly because of their tax-exempt status. But today this traditional immunity creates inequities which endanger the future of the churches and of American society. *For this reason, I believe churches must seriously examine their privileged position to see whether they should not offer some modifications to taxing authorities.*

The adage that "the power to tax is the power to destroy" is true. It is also true that the churches may be destroyed by their tax exemptions.

Today our churches own a great deal of tax-exempt property, pay no inheritance taxes, and own and operate businesses without paying the 52 percent corporate income tax. Assuming prudent management—and recalling what has happened in other countries —I could reasonably prophesy that American churches might dominate the national economy within a century. That is a point to which I'll return, but—first—let me speak of a moral issue involved.

As Christians, we must question the justice of churches competing at an economic advantage against taxpaying citizens while availing themselves of all the benefits of government. We also must ask whether the churches' invasion of commercial arenas undermines the grounds on which their tax exemptions are based.

The government grants exemptions to certain properties on the theory that it is socially advantageous not to tax them. Thus, churches are exempted on the ground that they are desirable social undertakings. Some denominations seek additional justification on the ground that they conduct activities which would otherwise be

* The following article was written in 1962.

supported by the government, but this seems to be better justification of exemptions for hospitals, colleges, and parochial schools.

Still, most of us will agree that churches should be aided and encouraged to the limits of propriety. However, privileges which were necessary and proper when churches were small, poor, and weak may have unfortunate results when churches are large, rich, and powerful.

It is obvious to any taxpayer that too much tax-exempt property creates serious problems for governments beset by a population explosion. Cities are struggling to find new sources of revenue to meet the growing needs for police and fire protection, schools, and social welfare.

Since the biggest exemptions go to schools and government properties, it is clear that eliminating all religious exemptions would not solve the revenue problem. Nevertheless, if churches continue to accumulate land and businesses, the problem could become explosive. Revolutionary expropriation of church properties was the solution resorted to in sixteenth-century England, eighteenth-century France, nineteenth-century Italy, and twentieth-century Russia. Mexico still suffers social convulsions from such a seizure.

Hard-pressed governments sooner or later will turn on wealthy churches, and a wave of anticlericalism and atheism always precedes the clash. Such feeling already is apparent in the United States. It has not yet reached the dangerous stage, but it is growing steadily.

In an age when we build sprawling suburban homes and towering monuments to commerce, we would be less Christian than we are if we did not want to build great and beautiful churches. Yet the fact remains that an expensive church has an ambiguous effect on those outside the membership.

Monumental buildings—or even social welfare and educational projects—are not enough to make a poor man love a rich church. If they are financed by profits resulting from special privilege, they are more likely to earn envy and hatred.

This is the visible part of the problem, but there is an equal threat from within. I am sure that the concentration of wealth and power in the hands of the churches eventually will only frustrate the very ends which they proclaim and profess. At least I have seen nothing to indicate that church leaders supported by huge endowments and mounting investments will conduct themselves in a more Christian manner than those scraping the bottom of the financial barrel.

Lest it seem that the threat of our churches becoming preoccupied with financial matters lies entirely in the future, let me point out that rich men already are encouraged to give big gifts to churches, since these gifts cost them little or nothing. And church trustees are offered deals whereby they buy a business and then lease it back to the original owners, thus securing a tax advantage for both parties.

I believe the churches should move at once to end all such abuses. We could begin by giving up the exemption from the corporate tax on income from business unrelated to the religious purpose of the church. We also could take the initiative in approaching local authorities and discussing the possibility of placing our land and buildings on the tax rolls. We might work out a system whereby we could voluntarily make partial payment in lieu of taxes which would pay our share of the cost of streets and police and fire protection.

I do not pretend to have the final answer to so complex a problem. It is sometimes very difficult to tell when a religious-book publishing house ceases to be an extension of the church and becomes a commercial enterprise. And while the small-town or rural church might easily afford the going property tax rate, churches in downtown New York City or Chicago could not.

I would regard any policy which drives the churches off all the good corners in our great cities as excessive, but I do believe that something must be done. We must seriously ask ourselves whether Christianity's lofty goals are not severely compromised by our tax exemptions.

Chapter 15

THE CHURCHES AND
COMMUNISM*

IT was Adolf Hitler who perfected first the technique of the "big lie." He proved that falsehood repeated enough could brainwash a whole people, no matter how absurd the falsehood might appear to the rational mind.

Some of our presbyteries, along with their churches, are being subjected to the "big lie" technique by the current rash of charges that the churches, particularly Protestant churches, and the ministry, particularly Protestant ministers, have been widely infiltrated by communism.

Louis Cassels of United Press International wrote in the New York *World-Telegram* and elsewhere on April 29, 1961:

> FBI Director J. Edgar Hoover is deeply concerned about the danger that self-appointed "vigilantes" may, in the name of anti-communism, play into communists' hands.
>
> During the past few weeks, Mr. Hoover has sent FBI Chief Inspector William C. Sullivan to deliver speeches in many parts of the nation, warning Americans not to be taken in by charges that their churches are overrun by Reds.
>
> "These allegations have served to create the impression among many Americans that the Protestant denominations in particular have been subjected to alarming infiltration and influence," Mr. Sullivan says.
>
> "But this is a patent falsehood. The truth is that the Communist Party has not achieved any substantial success in exerting domination, control, or influence over America's clergymen or religious institutions on a national scale."

Mr. Cassels continues:

* The following talk was delivered to the Presbytery of Los Angeles on May 9, 1961.

Mr. Sullivan is not making this statement on his own authority. He is speaking with the full approval and personal backing of Mr. Hoover. And the FBI director has so informed a number of amateur Communist hunters who wrote him protesting Mr. Sullivan's speeches.

I know of no stronger third-party evidence that I can quote to make it perfectly clear that the widespread allegations of communist infiltration of the Protestant ministry or the leadership of our Church or of the National Council of Churches is brazen falsehood. If any of you have been worried by these charges, I hope you are convinced. And may I go further and remind you that repeating these slanders and libels or even gossiping about them makes you an accessory to the conspiracy which is attempting to weaken the influence of your pulpits, your churches, and your councils, locally and nationally.

I remind you that we have traced these lies to their sources. I do not intend to list them for you again, since nothing pleases these "apostles of discord" more than to receive publicity, which they cannot get on their own, when a churchman names them. Of all the letters I received after my sermon of last winter in Santa Barbara on this same topic (see chapter 16) was one from one of these sources of falsehood, complaining that I had left him out of my listing. My reason was that he and his pamphlets were not listed on the single sheet of calumny that formed the basis of my sermon outline, the text of which was "Thou shalt not bear false witness against thy neighbor." He should have made his complaint to the anonymous cowards who printed and circulated the poison sheet to the members of the First Presbyterian Church of Santa Barbara. But we can identify quite easily the original sources of the lies. You can tell your people that the chances are better than ten to one that any church story is false that is datelined Tulsa, Oklahoma; Collingswood, New Jersey; Madison, Wisconsin; Cincinnati, Ohio; or Wheaton, Illinois. Most of the alleged facts, which go back to the McCarthy era or earlier, have been denied and disproved again and again.

How is it then that they still trouble us? Partly because the big lie technique does not depend on facts. But partly now because the old lies are being actively circulated by the same people who were McCarthy's stooges a few years ago, but are now reorganized into typical totalitarian cells of disruption under a retired candy manufacturer of the Commonwealth of Massachusetts.

The illogic of this whole campaign has been illustrated again and again by the man's own words. In effect he says that you can't trust anybody, not the President, nor the State Department, not the army, not any politicians, certainly not the newspapers, or the preachers; *therefore* trust him. His argument to trust him is that he has "a nose for communists."

When his more-than-usually fantastic charge was publicized that former President Eisenhower was a communist, even most of his followers realized he had gone too far, but their lack of logic and common sense made them say, "I don't agree that President Eisenhower is a communist, but mostly I still agree." When a totalitarian scoundrel is caught charging falsely that one distinguished patriot is a communist, or communist dupe, the only logical conclusion is not, "he has gone too far," but rather, "this proves that he does not in any respect know what he is talking about."

The other reason for the current increase in the circulation and acceptance of these false charges about communist infiltration is the fact that, generally speaking, the American people are frightened. Things have not been going well in the "cold war." Cuba and Laos have taken a good deal of hope and confidence from the American people. Berlin threatens. This real ground of fear of communist success is a fertile field for planting seeds of distrust. We are all happy to find a scapegoat.

Let me repeat what I have often said and most deeply believe. Free pulpits and free churches all across this land are the best bulwark against communism that the nation owns.

I am not really fearful that our Church will be mortally hurt by the attacks against us. What I do fear is that we will become so busy defending ourselves that we will not make the contribution we should to true Americanism in our several communities and in the nation as a whole. Our churches in every community should be inspiring the community to support the United Nations as man's best hope for peace and freedom. Our churches in every community should be taking the lead in support of the public schools against those who are trying to disrupt them by making false charges against the best and most conscientious teachers we have. Our churches should be busy preaching the gospel of Jesus Christ, the good news of God that alone will give us the courage to face the real threats to our nation and our culture and civilization.

I urge you to get off the defensive and, in every church, to begin the attack that our nation needs to be protected from those who, in their fear of communism, would destroy American freedom.

If these attackers of freedom have infiltrated Presbyterian sessions, the presbytery has the power and duty to go in to the support of courageous preachers, who will preach the truth. If these enemies of freedom have infiltrated our membership, sessions have the power and duty to discipline members who slander the Church of Jesus Christ by false charges of communism.

Now it is true that our gospel is not always popular. It is true that some of our members and even our officers may be worried to hear the Christian gospel preached. But I urge you ministers and elders not to be afraid to stand for your faith. Let me suggest what our biblical faith is—even though I shall have time to set it forth in outline only.

1. All Christians worthy of the name believe in God as revealed in Jesus Christ. If we really believe in the sovereign living God, why should the communist conspiracy or its totalitarian and fascist cousins make us afraid? Let us encourage our people to trust God, speak the truth, and believe in the victory of righteousness that Christ has already won.

2. All Christians worthy of the name know that love rather than hate is the most powerful weapon. Let us remember that Jesus said, "Love your enemies." Let us not be afraid to preach Christ even if some will charge us with being weak or stupid. What hope has the Christian pulpit of being respected if the preacher is afraid to preach biblical truth? What else are you preachers paid your salaries for? Will you let your pulpits become soft echoes of the worst prejudices of your people?

3. All Christians worthy of the name know that the Christian faith is not simply an American faith, but one which is worldwide. Stand up for the United Nations. Make clear why you hate communist ideology, but don't hate the Russian people, or even the Soviet government. Tell your people why from Christian grounds we ought to help the poor nations out of our abundance. Remind them that the Christian faith is concerned about all men—Russians, Latin Americans, Negroes, Mexicans, as well as stupid and

decadent white Protestants. Don't pull your punches. Some will get into trouble—for sure—so did Jesus Christ. Don't let the doctors make you afraid to challenge them to provide better medical care for old people. Don't let your realtors keep you silent about housing or about open covenants of occupancy for all races. Do you think we dare let the communists be the only friends of the poor and the hungry and the disinherited?

Surely be persuasive if you can. But don't expect that the gospel will ever win you a popularity contest.

In addition to these general Christian truths that we are obligated to preach, let us remember our Presbyterian heritage and stand up for it as well.

We Presbyterians believe that constitutional representative government is the right way for free men to govern themselves under God in both Church and State. Don't let anybody get away with challenging that heritage in the Presbyterian Church.

We Presbyterians believe that our religion, both individual and corporate, ought to bear upon the whole realm of human life. Don't let anybody silence you or make you afraid to apply the gospel to economics, politics, social ethics, or anything else that is controversial.

We Presbyterians believe in a sovereign God, strong enough to accomplish His will in the face of Satan and all his cohorts. Let's begin to behave as if we did believe it. Surely we are not promised that such a course will be easy or pleasant or successful. We don't know what God's will may be for us. But we do know that if we are faithless in our times of trial, there is no hope but that God Himself must repudiate us as faithless servants.

Let's move in to the battle. Let us so behave that the world may note what we say and do and perhaps be drawn to Jesus Christ, because they see that we are His.

Chapter 16

THE NATIONAL COUNCIL OF CHURCHES
AND THE FAR RIGHT*

I CALL to your attention that this commandment warns us against a very specific form of untruth, namely, lying about your fellows. I am asked to come and preach to you in Santa Barbara today because this congregation is being subjected to a campaign of false witness about the leadership of your Church, both lay and ministerial, and about the leadership of the National Council of Churches.

Although the campaign of false witness is apparently directed against the leaders of your denomination and their associates from other denominations in the National Council of Churches, I pause to remind you that the attack is as much against the Presbyterian Church of Santa Barbara, your own session, and your own pastor. I have come here this morning therefore not to defend myself or my associates on the General Board of the National Council of Churches, except incidentally, but to help you see what certain persons and outside organizations are trying to do to you and your particular church.

Let me begin by an analysis of the eight questions recently circulated to this congregation on a single sheet of paper headed "Attention: Members of the Presbyterian Church of Santa Barbara." Under boldface large print "Do you know—" you were in this sheet asked eight questions. The question technique is suggested, by the way, in the *Blue Book* of the John Birch Society as the best way to sow disruption and to disturb a church or P.T.A.

"Do you know that your church is a member of the National Council of Churches?"

---

* The following sermon was preached March 19, 1961, at the Presbyterian Church of Santa Barbara, California, on the text: "Thou shalt not bear false witness against thy neighbor" (Exodus 20:16).

If by Church is meant the United Presbyterian Church in the U.S.A., the answer to the question is a clear "yes." If, however, you turned over the page you read these words in black boldface type: "The Rebellion of the People Who Pay the Bills Is On!" On this page then is printed a resolution of a Houston church designed to promote a widespread attack on the policies and leaders of the National Council of Churches.

The final paragraph illustrates best of all the lengths to which these people will go to discredit the leaders of your churches.

"Officers of the National Council, World Council of Churches, who make up the Central Committee of the World Council of Churches met in Nyborg, Denmark August 23, 1959 to define what Christians should do about the threat of atomic war."

In the first place the Central Committee of the World Council of Churches is made up of ninety representatives of denominations Protestant and Orthodox and not of the officers of the National Council of Churches. A clear attempt is made in this sentence to make you think that the National Council of Churches and the World Council of Churches are responsible for each other's actions. The paragraph continues: "A report which received mild criticism declared Christians should find surrender preferable to all-out war. If all-out war should occur, Christians should urge 'cease-fire,' if necessary on the enemies' terms, and resort to nonviolent resistance."

The purpose of this sentence is to imply that the World Council of Churches and the National Council hold the position of pacifism in the face of the undoubted threat of communist world domination. It is simply not so. I was at the meeting referred to. The World Council did not approve any report which took such a position. Here was a report before the committee which was a serious study of what Christians should do under the threat of atomic war. This is a subject that needs discussion. But the fact is that no position was approved—certainly not that which this lying propaganda sheet implies. And I remind you that if it had, it is hardly honest to confuse what a world body does with the actions of the National Council of Churches.

The next question on the propaganda sheet distributed to you was:

"Do you know that your local church cannot withdraw if it

wished from the National Council and that your local church is
not owned by the congregation?"

Let us analyze that question. The reason you as a local church
cannot withdraw from the National Council is because as a local
church you are not a member. The National Council of Churches
is a council of denominations. The United Presbyterian Church in
the U.S.A. is, as you ought to know, one Church with more
than nine thousand particular churches or congregations.

But the second part of the question is even more confusing.
You are asked whether you know that your local church is not
owned by the congregation? This will be a surprise to your board
of trustees. The property of this church is owned by the California
Corporation known as the Presbyterian Church of Santa Barbara
and held according to its by-laws and will continue to be held
by it unless and until it might be proved that the local leadership
of this church, its elders, had broken their ordination vows and
were leading the congregation out of the United Presbyterian
Church in the U.S.A. by subverting its constitution. The implication of this second part of question 2 is a flat lie.

The paper continues: "Do you know the National Council
maintains a political lobby in Washington, D.C.?"

The true answer to that question is "No." I quote from the
by-laws of the Washington office committee of the National
Council, of which at one time I was chairman.

The Washington office serves both member churches and Council
units in the following ways: "Gives prompt and authoritative
notice regarding pending legislative governmental activities, and
other development in the capitol affecting the functioning of the
churches and their agencies; secures official interpretations of legislative and administrative acts when required; indicates channels
for contacts in Washington and furnishes facilities for affecting
them when desired. The office is not to engage in efforts to influence legislation; coordinates activities in relation to governmental
agencies carried on by Council representatives in Washington."

I remind you that the propaganda sheet we are analyzing implies
that the Washington office is a political lobby. I ask you sincerely
whether you would not rightly be critical of the national leadership
of your Church and its councils if we had no regular channels to
and from Washington for the purposes just now described.

How do you think we could get passports and visas for the thousands of foreign missionaries of our churches if we had no channel of communication to the State Department and the foreign embassies? Do you think our work in the inner cities with juvenile delinquency would be better if we knew nothing about U.S. Government activities in this field? Or how would we have been able to cooperate with the U.S. Government in distributing more than 15 million dollars worth of surplus foods last year through Church World Service (a department of the National Council of Churches) if we had no Washington office? Or do you think it would be good for the country if the Protestant and Orthodox churches did not have their six-person staff in Washington while the National Catholic Welfare Conference (headquarters of the Roman Catholic Church) continues to have a staff of 250 people at 1312 Massachusetts Ave., N.W., Washington, D.C.?

I could stop here and go on to the next question but I want to be entirely fair. One of the criticisms of the National Council of Churches is that it from time to time makes pronouncements on political and social and economic matters. There are some within our churches who feel that it would be much better if we never entered this field at all. Let us look very carefully at this question. First you should know that 95 percent of the budget and 75 percent of staff time of the National Council has to do with evangelism, relief, foreign missions, Christian education—activities that receive very little newspaper or TV publicity because they are not controversial.

But I ask you to think with me for a few minutes about this question. Should the Protestant and Orthodox churches keep entirely silent, as if they did not care about the legislation that is proposed in Washington? Would you really like that?

"Do you know that many of the pronouncements of the National Council are extremely socialistic and radical in concept, and that these pronouncements are made in your name even though you may disagree?"

The answer to that question is that to label pronouncements extremely radical or socialistic is a good way to make you stop thinking and become emotional.

Let me take an example of the controversial statement on medical care for the aged approved by the General Board on February 23 in Syracuse:

The voluntary sharing among groups of people of the risks and hazards of illness, and the voluntary pooling of some of their funds to meet the cost of care for any in their group who may need it is indeed a Christian approach to this problem, whether this method is utilized by churches, labor unions, industrial managements, fraternal organizations, cooperatives, community groups, or by subscribers for health insurance. The National Council of Churches commends it and urges its widest possible application.

Do those sentences sound radical or socialistic? I freely admit that is not all the statement said. I have a good friend, a surgeon, with whom I was discussing this whole matter on February 20. We disagreed rather violently on the subject. He is a Presbyterian. I have another friend, a Presbyterian elder who is perhaps the outstanding expert on Social Security and old age retirement in our Church. He agrees with the statement. I am quite sure that in this very congregation there would be sharp disagreement on some of these issues if we took time to debate them. One of the sad things is that on the whole the poorer of you would likely turn out to be supporters of Social Security and the richer likely to be against it. Do not you both then need to study the matter carefully in the light of the Christian faith and gospel? It is this kind of study that the National Council of Churches is set up to give us. But if you let these propagandists have their way they will divide this church right down the middle between "communists" and "fascists," hating each other, labeling each other, and distrusting each other.

As to the implication of the second part of the question: "Do you know that the pronouncements are made in your name even though you may disagree?" That is untrue. False. Here is what the recent General Assembly of the National Council of Churches at San Francisco said about the Council's pronouncements:

> . . . this Council under its Constitution is basically governed by a Triennial Assembly made up of the elected representatives of the churches. These representatives are sent here to deliberate and decide upon matters regularly brought before them by members, churches and by representative committees or departments or divisions. In this restricted sense, and in this sense only, every act of this Assembly is representative of the thirty-four churches which compose the Council and of their forty million members.

The pronouncements, resolution, and other actions of a General

Assembly have precisely the status and weight of being actions of such a representative assembly; no more, no less. They will be useful as they serve as a guide and help to the churches and their members and to the nation and the world, in finding God's will and doing it.

And earlier the General Board made the official statement:

The General Board of the National Council of Churches reminds the churches that its pronouncements, policy statements, and findings of study conferences are designed to help our members in the free process of finding the truth and acting upon it. They are not to be interpreted as beyond thoughtful criticism.

The one-page sheet of propaganda circulated to you continues: "Do you know that the Revised Standard Version of the Bible is copyrighted by the National Council and that 30 of the 95 men who gave us the RSV have had communist front affiliations?"

I can answer the first part of that question by asking a parallel one. Do you know that every new translation of the Bible is copyrighted by someone as is every expensive book in order that pirated editions may not be published without paying the publishers and editors for their years of work that made it possible?

As for the second part of the question, the answer is "No." Not true. This is flat false witness. I quote from the chairman of the committee, Dr. Luther A. Weigle, as his statement appears in the *Congressional Record* of April 19, 1960. Dean Weigle was accused in the pamphlet which is the source of these lies of affiliation with six communist-front organizations. This is Dean Weigle's signed statement.

Let me take the case of myself as an individual, for it chances that I have been named by some attackers. I am not and have not been a Communist; I do not belong and have not belonged to any Communist-front organizations. Specifically, I have not been a member of any of the organizations that I have seen to be named in any of these attacks upon me; I have never attended a meeting of any of these organizations and I have not contributed to them; I have never been cited before any committee of Congress dealing with un-American activities. To turn the statement around and put it positively, I am in politics a Republican, in theology a Lutheran, and in my ecclesiastical connection and ministerial office, a Congregationalist.

I have known Dean Weigle for twenty-five years and know that he is a gentleman and a scholar.

The false witness of the propaganda sheet distributed to the members of this congregation continues:

"Do you know that the immediate past president of the National Council, Edwin T. Dahlberg, has a record of numerous communist fronts?"

This is a general charge that is difficult to deal with. The Rev. Dr. Dahlberg, a pastor in St. Louis, Missouri, did have affiliation with certain organizations which were later—much later—taken over by the communists. When Russia was our ally in fighting Germany and Japan, Dr. Dahlberg belonged to one organization, now listed as communist-affiliated, which, however, when he was a member had in its membership General Eisenhower, Ambassador Davies, and a host of other Americans who were loyal then and remained loyal until now or their death. Dr. Dahlberg is no more a communist or a dupe of communists than Presidents Roosevelt, Truman, Eisenhower, or Kennedy or candidates Willkie, Dewey, or Nixon, although all have been accused at one time or other as having been soft on communists or duped by them.

The false witness continues:

"Do you know that there is a plan to merge the four largest denominations in the United States, the Presbyterian Church being one of the denominations, and that thereafter the National Council would speak and lobby for you whether you agree or not?"

Since the question refers clearly to a sermon I preached in Grace Cathedral in San Francisco on December 4, 1960, I think you may accept me as something of an expert on the subject. My full sermon was printed in the January 1, 1961, issue of *Presbyterian Life* and I ask you to read it. First, let me say that no one, not Bishop Pike, no other preacher, no organization, has any connection with or responsibility for that sermon but myself.

When I preached it, I did not know that it would attract the wide attention and approval that it has. As of this date twenty-seven presbyteries of our Church have asked the General Assembly by resolution or overture to make it official.

Whether such a union as I proposed will ultimately find favor with God or man I do not know. But to use it as an attack upon the National Council of Churches and to imply by the question that it is some kind of conspiracy to put you in the control of the Council is false witness and breaks the Ninth Commandment.

Finally the propaganda of false witness asks:

"Do you know what the Ecumenical movement is and what it portends?"

If you did know the truth about the Ecumenical Movement and its councils I would not have had to preach this sermon. How do you find out the truth? Read what the councils do and say in their own publications. Don't let people lie about them to you by innuendo such as I have just analyzed.

How do they want you to find out more? They list eleven publications. Three of these are by Carl McIntire, who was by judicial process deposed from the Presbyterian ministry in 1936, because he was one of a group of people bearing false witness then about the Board of Foreign Missions of our Church. He followed those who were attacking Dr. Robert P. Speer and Dr. Charles R. Erdman and were saying that they were modernists. After being deposed because of bearing false witness and breaking his ordination vows, Dr. McIntire has spent all this quarter-century attacking the Church which reluctantly had to discipline him. He found he could make little progress attacking the Church which he had left, so he began to attack its leaders as being "soft on communism." This has been more successful but just as false.

Two of the publications listed for you in which to read more of this poison are by Dr. Edgar Bundy of Wheaton, Illinois. Dr. Bundy is a self-styled patriot who is the source of much of the falsehood I have been describing. Let me give you an example. The October, 1958, issue of his *News and Views* is wholly devoted to an attack on me implying that I am a communist, soft on communism, or a communist dupe. This is false witness. It is true that I believe segregation of Negroes is unchristian and un-American and that I believe government should use force in any part of the nation to repress violence against the law of the land. In this I take the position as reluctantly but as firmly as did Abraham Lincoln one hundred years ago. It is true that I visited the leaders of the churches in the Soviet Union in March, 1956, as the leader of a group of churchmen in the United States. On the delegation were the then most distinguished Protestant Church leaders of this land. That trip and its consequences have been most valuable in reestablishing relationships with the Christian

Churches behind the iron curtain. My going there makes me no more a communist or soft on communism or a dupe of communism than it does Dick Nixon or President Eisenhower. I have not time to take up the six pages of false witness about me. Nor is it necessary. I am a Presbyterian, a Republican, and what I believe about God and Jesus Christ is public knowledge from sermons preached in free pulpits all over this land for nearly thirty years.

These McIntires and Bundys cannot hurt wholly me or my reputation. But they can hurt a host of young Presbyterian preachers who are attacked by such organizations as those of McIntire and Bundy, and now the John Birch Society, by these campaigns of falsehood. I urge these young men to stand up to attack the falsehoods as I have been doing today. I urge this congregation to become awake as to what these "apostles of discord" are trying to do to you and your Church.

One of the publications recommended in the propaganda sheet of falsehood circulated among you is published by Circuit Riders, Inc., an organization that is trying to disrupt the Methodist Church. I refer you to Bishop Kennedy of that Church for his comment on that organization and I do this despite the fact that according to the press Bishop Kennedy is the most outspoken Methodist critic of the plan of union to which I have referred.

Another of the publications you are asked to read is published by Billy James Hargis, former minister of the Christian Churches in Tulsa, Oklahoma, who is vicious and inaccurate in his attacks on the National Council of Churches. I am happy that until now I know nothing of the authors of the other publications listed with the exception of the last, which, strange to say, is a publication of the National Council of Churches itself. I hope you will read it. It is a full report of the Cleveland Study Conference which has been so widely attacked. Read it and you will see that those who have attacked it and the National Council of Churches and its leaders through it have distorted it out of recognition. And it should be noted it is a study document and not a pronouncement of a National Council of Churches' "political" position. So I say read and study it.

Let me conclude with my text. "Thou shalt not bear false witness against thy neighbor." Why is this important? Principally because it is one of the Ten Commandments given to us by God through the Holy Bible. Secondarily, it is important because false witness is the only way a free people can be persuaded to give up their liberty, destroy their institutions, and fall prey to one or another kind of totalitarian dictatorship. If there appears in this congregation real difference of conviction about any matter touched on in this sermon, I suggest your session proceed to handle it under the law and constitution of your Church.

Just as America will be saved only as she adheres to law and her Constitution, so also will your Church continue to be one of the strongest bulwarks for freedom in the nation and the world as she is associated in the councils of the Ecumenical Movement under the lordship of Jesus Christ.

The New Ecumenical
Reformation

❧❧

Chapter 17

THAT CONTROVERSIAL ECUMENICAL MOVEMENT, 1965 *

THE Ecumenical Movement is a Christian movement. It should not be understood simply in terms of tolerance, good will, and syncretism, the latter of which is the basic typical attitude of Western culture toward religion. It has at its heart a deep measure of good will toward all men of whatever faith or conviction, but it is opposed to an easy tolerance of theological or philosophical differences, as if conviction or faith really did not matter. It resists a too easy effort to find too simple formulae of agreement.

The Ecumenical Movement must not be confused with structures, organizations, or programs of the various Christian churches —Protestant or Catholic. It should be understood as the cause of the World Council of Churches, the Second Vatican Council, the National Councils of Churches in many lands, church union proposals and accomplishments. Some people erroneously think almost the exact opposite, namely, that the Councils of Churches caused and promote the Ecumenical Movement.

The movement is worldwide (ecumenical) and may be defined as consisting of the ideas, convictions, and personal relationships that arise out of faith in the one Lord Jesus Christ.

It may also be defined in terms of three words, the first of which is "unity." Let me indicate briefly what most ecumenical churchmen mean when they speak of the unity of the Church of Jesus Christ.

The Church is one. Unity is not something to be promoted. It is given by the Lord of the Church. Obedience to Jesus Christ

---

* The following essay was written for the *Lawrentian*, a publication of the Lawrenceville School, Lawrenceville, New Jersey, from which Dr. Blake was graduated in 1924. Its purpose was to explain the Ecumenical Movement to the lay alumni of that institution.

requires a Catholic, an Anglican, an Eastern Orthodox, a Presbyterian, a Methodist, a Baptist, or whatever, to try to make manifest to the world the given unity of the Church, not to create it.

In order to manifest this unity, Christians of every kind are compelled to cooperate so far as truth and conscience allow with all other Christians with their churches (usually in councils). In order to manifest this unity, churchmen must continually examine possibilities of reunion of Christian churches and work for visible community and union.

Ecumenists take the position that if this effort is not made, the gospel is distorted, the churches are all weakened, and the public scandal of division is advertised.

This is not to be understood as the repudiation of his fathers in the faith by anyone. The Ecumenical Movement takes history seriously. And what is more serious than the one thousand years of separation between Eastern and Western Christianity during most of which a cold war was going on between East and West? Or what is more serious than five hundred years of the fragmentation of Christianity in the West, initiated by the Reformation?

Ecumenists believe that it is our present task to be obedient to Jesus Christ, the one Lord, that under Him the same faith and loyalty which caused the tragic divisions of the one Church might now reunite them. Our fathers divided because of their concern for the truth and relevance of the gospel of Jesus Christ. The central concern of ecumenism is the same.

In these past fifty years we have witnessed the turning of a tide that flowed unchecked toward division for over a thousand years. No one yet can foresee the shape of unity to come, but only a blind man could suppose that nothing important is happening in the field of church unity.

The second ecumenical word is "renewal." Ecumenical Christians believe that unity will be a disaster unless it is accompanied by the renewal of the Church under the spirit of God.

The world outside has long been radically critical of the churches. There is nothing written today more radically critical of the churches as they are than that which is written by ecumenical Christians from inside them, with the single exception of those who don't believe in God, or in any religion. This criticism of the churches from within is based essentially on two charges: institutionalism and provincialism. Ecumenists generally agree that the churches, as organized, too often allow their organizations to stand in the way of the purpose of the organization. The balanced budget too easily becomes the crucial test of the church's "success." The number of members seems to become more important than what happens to the members. Personal power within the organization and the power of the organization in the world become more important to the churches' leaders than obedience to Jesus Christ. Churches become ends in themselves, representing the morality of their members, instead of being agents of God representing God's morality to the members.

And churches are provincial, geographically and denominationally, and representative of a single class or race. In the United States this can easily be seen. We have seen the Roman Catholics as Irish or Italian or Polish culture churches. The Presbyterians are a Scots or Scotch-Irish clan. Episcopalians are upper-class British, with their hangers-on. Lutherans are German or Scandinavian clubs. The great Negro denominations are the only institutions that they have been allowed to own and run for themselves. All the churches are alienated from the truly poor.

The Ecumenical Movement has been from the beginning a strong force against this tendency in all the churches. This is the reason why the churches have become involved in the racial crisis in the United States. Unless the Christian Church is able to press upon its members the requirement that they should lead in the establishment of just patterns of racial and social justice, not only will the nation lose all its idealism, but the churches themselves will be revealed as barren and fruitless.

Furthermore we are now entering into an age of universal history. No longer is Selma, Alabama, unimportant to Peking, or vice versa. It is one world technically, economically, and, increasingly, politically. In order to escape provincialism, the churches must transcend the nations and even the continents where they have their roots. This is why the World Council of Churches received in 1961 a new large bloc of members from the nations in the Soviet orbit. The Church of Jesus Christ to be the Church cannot remain the instrument of American foreign policy. This is essentially why the Ecumenical Movement is controversial. It challenges the basic assumptions of all men everywhere that national patriotism and national survival are the highest human values.

One may sum up this section of this essay by saying flatly: "The Ecumenical Movement is trying to reform and transform every church and denomination from a culture club into God's agency or reconciliation to Himself and among all men to each other."

Finally, the third ecumenical word is "mission." I use the word here in the military sense rather than in the traditional Church sense, though I shall come to that at the end.

Some years ago, when I was president of the National Council of Churches, I paid a Christmas visit to the troops at Thule in the far north of Greenland. As I remember it, there were some ten thousand men stationed in that cold, twenty-four-hour darkness. Why were they there? Most of them were struggling to keep each other warm, housed, fed, and entertained. The *mission* of the base was to keep at twenty-four-hour alert a small wing of fighter planes to intercept any bomber force which might be sent across the pole from Russia to attack the United States. The Christian Church, without its mission, could very well be compared to the Thule military base without any fighter planes.

What is the mission of the Church? It is to proclaim by word and act the good news to all men that God was in Jesus Christ reconciling the whole world to Himself. Unless the Church is doing that job, it had better be liquidated. History does not reveal a pretty story about the Church. Again and again in various crises, the Church has been false to God and betrayed the true saints among its members.

The Ecumenical Movement aims to save the Church in the twentieth century from the tragedies of the past, praying and working to make it a more effective instrument for the purposes of God. That is a rather large order. Yet the alternatives to faith, hope, and love are still as they have always been: cynicism, despair, and hate. Each of us who has been educated enough to be a leader in any area of our common life is challenged to decide which way he will choose to throw his influence.

Chapter 18

_____

CRISIS IN THE MINISTRY *

THE United Presbyterian Church in the United States of America faces a crisis in the morale of many of its pastors and in the recruiting of young men to become pastors chiefly because it is no longer certain about what a pastor is or should be.

When I was a young man in college and in the process of deciding whether or not I had a call to the ministry, I was not sure whether I wanted to be a pastor or a teacher. In fact I did not make the decisive choice until three years out of seminary. In what respects was my indecision in this similar to that of young men in college or university today, and in what respects dissimilar?

It was similar in that students of all generations tend to lean toward teaching, since the most creative environment to develop thoughts and values that most of them have known has been in school and college rather than in home or church. It is not surprising that I, over thirty years ago, and students now in school and college are much alike in that we tend to be drawn favorably to an intellectual and cultural life we know. Most of the good students in any school contemplate the possibility of teaching.

But there are at least two attitudes apparently held by many students today that, so far as I remember, we did not hold thirty years ago. Most students today apparently hold an anti-institutional bias which did not so affect us. Like all youth, we were critical of our elders and were quite certain we would do better than they, but we were not deeply affected by what is apparently a widespread conviction of youth today that all institutions get in the way of their professed purposes—a particularly embarrassing opinion when it is applied to an organized church.

* This address was written in 1963.

There is a second attitude held quite widely among students today which I believe is different from that held in my student generation: students today, even students who have begun to respond to a call from God to the Christian ministry, seem widely to have concluded that to be a pastor of a congregation, to preach, teach, and show concern for individuals and families, is a kind of work that would be both irrelevant to true Christian faith and dull to boot.

This does not mean that I did not have normal doubts about the churches I had seen and known. This does not mean that my generation was overromantic about the effectiveness or joy of a pastorate in a local church. It means rather that we looked forward to serving God as Presbyterian pastors in the way they had, so far as we knew, always done it.

Let me remind you that we did not think of the pastor as a church administrator who had minor responsibilities of leading in worship and offering pastoral care. We expected in a church to be preachers, who also led in worship, and pastors, that is, to call upon the people, marry them, baptize their children, and bury them. We did not know you had to be any kind of organization executive.

I was in fact so much uninterested in administration that I have sometimes wondered how I changed so much that I became a church administrator a dozen years ago. The most satisfying answer I have found is that being interested in every other part of my work—reading, writing, praying, calling, teaching—I learned to do administration quickly to get it out of the way.

This all leads me to one basic conclusion about the Presbyterian ministry. Unless we are able to recapture something of the enthusiasm and respect for what an "ordinary" pastor is and does, or to create a new and acceptable image of what he should be and do now, we are going to have a harder time recruiting young men for the pastorate before it becomes any easier. Let me analyze this into several parts:

1. Presbyterians must recapture a sense of the awe and mystery in connnection with the worship of God. I have a feeling that there has come to be so great a division in our own thinking about public worship and being a Christian that most Presbyterian pastors today are schizophrenic about their task.

2. In our highly organized society, pastors must learn to prize

the amazing amount of interest and freedom built into the pastorate (despite all the committee meetings and mimeographing) as contrasted with the routine and boredom of almost all jobs in mass business, education, and society.

3. Presbyterians must learn to prize the intimate personal relationships that arise from the sharing of joy and sorrow with human beings. A nephew of mine, trying to teach young physicians to be pediatricians, told me not long ago that most of his students didn't like people well enough to be good doctors. The psychological profiles of Presbyterian candidates for the ministry apparently indicate a similar problem.

4. Presbyterians must learn to distinguish between criticism of one another which is legitimate and might be helpful and that kind of undermining of one another—too common in our ministry —which reveals envy and malice.

Quite aside from any possible church union, there are a number of things going on in our Church now which may contribute to this recapturing of enthusiasm for the Presbyterian pastorate:

1. We are on the brink of a renewed understanding and practice of the public worship of God according to the best of our Reformed tradition in which biblical preaching will have its traditional important place but will not be the climax of the service.

2. We are struggling with the confessional position of our Church to the end that our ministers and ruling elders, who must make a confessional statement for ordination, may be released from the legalism in which our sole reliance on the Westminster Standards involves us. The plan of General Assembly's special committee, which it has reported to at least two General Assemblies, is to amend our confessional position by addition. The proposed additions are of two kinds: to include some of the sixteenth-century confessions which are more biblical; and to include at least one contemporary confession of our faith in the best Reformed and reforming tradition.

3. Another General Assembly special committee is examining church administration to see what modifications would be necessary to recapture the personal fellowship in the presbytery and the personal attention to the problems of churches and their pastors that our size and increased program complexities have tended to lose especially, but not exclusively, in the large metropolitan presbyteries.

4. Another committee is seeking to improve the method of examination of candidates so that in fact a better standard of qualifications for our ministry will be established by our presbyteries.

5. The General Council is attempting to coordinate the total general mission program of the denomination so that it will come to the pastor, not as an impossible complex of things he must do better than he has, but rather as an understandable direction and help for him to lead his congregation from wherever it is to a better instrumentality for obedience to Christ.

But I have been asked to write on this subject particularly in the light of the Ecumenical Movement and more specifically as it is related to possible church union.

It was because I believe that the full recapturing of the sense of mission of the Church in America, as well as its radical renewal, depends in part upon the recapturing of the visible unity of the Church, that I proposed the establishment of a united church in San Francisco. I still believe that the best and easiest way for our Church to revitalize and renew its ordained ministry would be to accomplish a broad union in a church "truly catholic, truly reformed, and truly evangelical."

When that time comes, the excitement about church union will begin again. The understanding of the nature of the ministry in such a united church is the key theological and political question. Most Presbyterians will traditionally react against any modification of our understanding of the ministry which leans in a Catholic direction. I can hear now the screams that will come from Nebraska and elsewhere if there is any re-examination of the concept of priest by us.

What I am suggesting here is that the whole first part of this paper really indicates that unless we do get some help from other churches, we have a problem in our Church which we can hardly hope to solve alone.

Our ministry has been so long based upon the attractive personality of the preacher pastor that we can hardly guess how much our Church and ministry would be helped by a renewal of the importance of worship which I judge will not likely come fully to us unless Catholic objectivity replaces some of the Protestant subjectivism that has tended to make our weekly worship unimportant and irrelevant.

This does not mean that we have nothing to give to our fellow churches in the Consultation. I am sure we have, but I am also sure that it is for others rather than ourselves to say what it is.

If we are to hope for a real revival of Church and ministry in America today, it will be by mutual enrichment and mutual correction.

I am not sure any of us are really ready for such a radical change. But lacking it, it is likely that the nature of the ministry will remain a problem rather than become once more a glorious affirmation of faith, hope, and obedience.

Chapter 19

PROPHET AND PRIEST,
BUT NOT KING*

I WANT to speak to you today about your ministry. As you are graduated from theological seminary this week, you go out from this place to your new places in the life of the Church. How you conceive of your ministry of word and sacrament will be important, not only as you begin it, but also all through your years of service to God and His people.

Much is said these days about the image of the Protestant minister. It is alleged that you young men are generally either confused about the ministry you are entering, or else that you resist the image of it that is most current. You are all familiar with the studies of Richard Niebuhr, which realistically describe the pastorate in the American Church. The new emphasis of this study is upon the administrative task that is laid upon the American pastor. Due to the multiplication of program activities even in the smaller churches, the "image" of the pastor has now come to be that of an executive of a social agency. He is expected to make the church "go" and his "success" seems to be measured by various statistics, such as new members received, money raised, buildings built, and the number of bustling programs conceived and promoted.

It is no wonder to me that many of you are hesitant and unsure of your calling if that is the way you conceive of it. But let us rather examine your ministry in theological terms in order that

---

* The following address was delivered to the graduating class of Princeton Theological Seminary in 1962, on the text: "And he said to them, 'The Kings of the Gentiles exercise Lordship over them; and those in authority over them are called Benefactors. But not so with you; rather let the greatest among you become as the youngest, and the leader as one who serves'" (Luke 22:25–26).

your image of the ministry may be enriched and the task you undertake in the Church seen in a fuller perspective.

It has become commonplace to say that the only ministry in the Church is Christ's ministry and that all other ministries are derivative from His. I have never quite fully understood the implications of this remark, which is usually uttered with a profundity that is supposed to *end* all argument. But let us *begin* our argument with it today.

Christ's ministry is *the* ministry in the Church. The ministry of the laity, that is of the whole people of God, including you and me, is the ministry of witnessing to Jesus Christ to which we were ordained by our baptism. So far so good. The specialized ministry of word and sacrament to which you and I have been called in the Church is derived from, and supportive of, both the ministry of Christ and that of all of the people of God. When we are ordained in and by the Church, our ministry is not new and different. The terms of the call of a minister in our Church—an essential part of his ordination—include these significant words: "that you may be free from worldly care and avocations." The reason a congregation undertakes to pay you a salary as pastor is neither to hire you to be something different from what you were before ordination, nor to signify any radical change in your ministry from that of the whole people of God. Rather you are freed by the Church for study and service and from the necessity of earning your livelihood in some "worldly" way.

To understand fully, then, what you are thus called to do and to be, it is necessary to look at Christ's own ministry as a model and pattern. In our tradition the ministry of Christ has been described usually as that of "prophet, priest, and King." Calvin writes in Book II, Chapter XV, of the *Institutes:* "The office enjoined upon Christ by the Father consists of three parts. For he was given to be prophet, King and priest." And in the Confession of Faith of our Church (VIII, I), one reads, "It pleased God, in his eternal purpose, to choose and ordain the Lord Jesus, his only begotten Son, to be the Mediator between God and man; the prophet, priest, and King. . . ."

If then the office of the minister of Jesus Christ is to be derived from Christ's own office in and to the Church, let us look at our ministry together today in terms of prophet, priest, and King. For as Calvin goes on to say in the *Institutes,* "It would be of little value to know these names without understanding their purpose and use."

In what sense then are you and I called by the Church to be prophets? Essentially, according to Calvin, a prophet is one who sets forth "useful doctrine sufficient for salvation" (see *Institutes,* Book II, Chapter XV). This broad definition will prevent us from too restricted an understanding of the prophetic role of the pastor and preacher. Some think of the prophet solely in terms of an Amos or a Jeremiah thundering "Thus saith the Lord" to a people unwilling to listen or to heed.

But it is much wiser to think of prophecy more broadly, as Calvin suggests, as setting forth the gospel, the good news of God in Christ, "sufficient for salvation." This will, of course, include "the social gospel," namely, the setting forth of the Word as it applies to the life of the Church and the world in terms that encourage the witness in the world of the people of God. But this is not easy to do, especially for a young man. Each of you by now has achieved some political, economic, and social orientation. Some of you are "liberals" in all of these. I doubt not that some of you are conservative, not to say reactionary. May I humbly suggest that the congregation to which you are called will be profoundly uninterested in your private views, liberal or conservative, on disarmament, integration, the profit system, or the United Nations. What your congregation has a right to hear from you is the gospel of Jesus Christ set forth in such clear fashion that as you preach, you and they together see the light of salvation in the pilgrim way you walk.

If you think of prophecy in these terms, you will find that you will not be speaking only as a counselor to fearful people, though you need to do that, nor only as a teacher of Christian doctrine, though you need to do that, nor only as a lone voice warning of God's judgment upon a faithless people, although every faithful preacher will be required from time to time to do that as well.

But salvation is no small thing. To speak God's Word of salvation to any people will require all of your knowledge and study, your humility and prayer, your continued learning and repeated moments of high courage.

The heart of what I am saying is that to be a true prophet of Jesus Christ and His gospel, the necessity is to undertake to speak on behalf of God to His people. This is no easy task. Brash young preachers more often get in trouble with their brashness than they do with the gospel. The broader and deeper your study of the gospel, the more humble you are about your own opinions and the surer you are about what God has done and is doing for man's salvation, the surer you are, week by week, to have something persuasive and important to say to the people to whom you are called to preach.

The danger of the preacher-prophet is when he begins for any reason to try to please man more than God, or when his righteous conviction is asserted as his own word to the people rather than God's. To be a prophet is an impossible task. Any minister of Christ who does not echo again and again in his own heart Jeremiah's protest at God's choosing him to be a prophet has not really begun his ministry. Jeremiah said, you remember, "Oh, Lord God! behold I do not know how to speak for I am only a youth." And thirty years from now, if you remain sensitive to your high calling, you will be protesting in your prayers, "Behold, I do not know how to speak for I am only a youth."

And as to Jeremiah, God's answer will be, "Do not say 'I am only a youth' . . . and whatever I command you, you will speak. . . . Behold I have put my words in your mouth."

God's words of reconciliation, courage, love, patience, judgment, and salvation—this is your high prophetic calling. No work is harder and no work more thrilling. If you so look at your ministry, you will not be confused, though you will know from the beginning that it is more than you, of your own ability and talent, can ever accomplish. And each Sunday you will pray that your words are God's words and that the salvation you proclaim is also His.

In what sense is a Presbyterian minister to be a priest? I am profoundly weary of the four-hundred-year-old disputes that continue to divide the Church of Jesus Christ on this matter. Of course, you are not a priest who controls the people's access to God. But no Catholic who knows his best tradition believes that either. Let us have done with ancient controversy and examine this ministry of ours in terms of Christ's ministry from which ours must be derived. Let us be very clear that Christ died upon a cross for our sins and for those of the whole world. This is His once-and-for-all accomplishment. He alone, after the order of Melchizedek, is prophet, *priest,* and King, the sole mediator between God and man. This we accept as having been accomplished. But positively why each week do the people of God gather in the sanctuary? Why are you called upon to lead this people to the throne of grace? In what sense is yours a priestly ministry? What is the relationship of cult to ethics or of worship to obedience?

If one were to put his finger on the chief source of the confusion of the American Protestant minister, it is just here. Most Presbyterian ministers are at a loss really to relate the regular worship of Almighty God, its hymns, prayers, and sacraments, to the scheme of salvation he sets forth in his preaching. This is the central sickness of the American Church today.

The cure to this sickness will not be found in our aping the outward acts of Catholic priests. Liturgical gadgets will not transform a Presbyterian service into anything useful. Reverence and worship cannot be produced by anything less than the consciousness of the presence of God Himself. But we as Presbyterian ministers do not believe that we in any sense control or contrive that presence. As our new *Directory for the Worship of God* puts it, "In worship the initiative lies with God. . . . In public worship God makes known among his people his love in Jesus Christ, his claim upon their lives, his abiding presence with them, and his concern for all creation. . . ." (W. II, 1), and our *Directory* also says, "Those ordained to the ministry of Word and Sacraments have entrusted to them the direction and leading of public worship" (W. I, 4).

This "Christian worship is . . . above all . . . a corporate response by the Church to God's mighty act of redemption in Jesus Christ" (W. II, 2).

If you and I will begin to think of our priestly office in these terms, there can be a resurgence of life and joy in the public worship of our Church. This task of leadership to which you are called is not the preliminary to your sermon. The worship of God in which the minister, with reverence, awe, and due preparation of mind and spirit, leads a congregation into the very presence of God is in our tradition the only setting for the effectual preaching of the Word.

I am told that many young men, sure of their call to Christ's ministry, are yet unsure of their call to serve as pastor of any particular church. "So much of what the churches do—budgets and Boy Scouts, building programs and dull social gatherings, women's associations and Sunday School picnics—what has this to do with my ministry?"

Let it be understood that every job in this world has its routine and uninteresting aspects. If any of you think my task in the Church is all glamor, think again. Hours of committee meetings and days and nights of travel, even abroad, soon lose their glamor. But what is more wonderful than week by week to enter a sanctuary, to lead a people who have come there voluntarily to worship God, to pray and sing, to voice praise and thanksgiving, to sit in Christ's place at His table, to preach the Word, and bless the people? If this is your work, cannot many small burdens be carried lightly with it?

The ministry of Word and sacrament in the Presbyterian Church is, in our increasingly organized and organizational life, one of the few callings which is centered in creative human and humane service. How can any young man resist a call to such a ministry? To compare it to being a cog in a great business, or even to prefer academic teaching to it, is profoundly to misconceive what the ministry may be in personal challenge and satisfaction, in deep joy and ultimate meaning.

But what about the minister being a King? You will have noticed that I named my sermon "Prophet and Priest, but *Not* King." By this topic I did not intend to imply that I would reject the third part of the traditional understanding of Christ's threefold ministry.

But I do want to make it clear that the idea that a Presbyterian minister is in any sense a "King" is false and misleading. In other days, when the parson was *the* person in a community, when discipline in the Church carried with it civil penalties, when, as in Geneva, Calvin sought order in a revolutionary age, there may have been excuse for making the pastorate appear to be at least a pale reflection of our Lord's rule in His Kingdom.

It is equally true that it is a profound misunderstanding of the present-day pastor's role if he is understood to be a boss or dictator of any kind, or an executive officer with authority over the people of his congregation.

Jesus said to His Disciples, "The Kings of the nations exercise Lordship over them; and those in authority over them are called Benefactors. But not so with you; rather let the greatest among you become as the youngest, and the leader as one who serves."

Surely the ministry of Word and sacrament is a kingly ministry too, if we will in our understanding of it accept Jesus' radical revolutionary view of lordship and rule.

I choose this text from Luke rather than the more familiar one in Matthew, particularly because I am speaking about our ministry to you young men. It is true that your youth, as you begin your ministry, is a handicap in your role of prophet, or of priest. The years add wisdom to the prophet and make his words more easily accepted; age and experience, sickness, sorrow, death—all these make a man a better priest. But here our Lord suggests that contrary to all the world's conception, a Christian King should be a youth, that is one who, because of junior status, finds it natural to be a servant—a minister.

So understood, the Kingly ministry is the willingness in obedience to our Lord to serve a whole congregation of people one by one. That is why, when you are tired, you will make that hospital call on a lonely invalid. That is why you will give yourself to the poor, the unlovable, the lonely, and the rich. That is why you will ring doorbells and call upon strangers, so that they may be no longer strangers.

We are told that the driving force in American life is status-seeking. I am sure all of us are human and ambitious enough to seek some status. But the status of a Christian minister is always a junior status, "Let the greatest among you become as the youngest, and the leader as one who serves."

If throughout your ministry you will remember this, in this sense only trying to retain your youth, you will find that this is an ambition which can be achieved. You will find that most of the heartache and most of the bitterness that has blighted men's ministries will not blight yours and that the end will be as thrilling as the beginning.

May such a ministry be yours. And if it is, it will be crowned by successive generations of young men in increasing numbers and quality who, having seen the reflection of our Lord in you, will also hear His call to serve Him in the Church.

Chapter 20

SECOND THOUGHTS ON
CHURCH UNION *

FOUR years ago last December 4, I preached a sermon from this pulpit which was "A Proposal Toward the Reunion of Christ's Church." Much has happened in these intervening years which bears upon that proposal for a step toward the reunion of the Church. I am happy, therefore, to have this opportunity to preach here again, this time on the subject "Second Thoughts on Church Union."

These second thoughts are not to be understood as either a reversal of the original proposal nor indeed a radical modification of it. I still believe that American churches ought to establish "a united church, truly catholic, truly reformed, and truly evangelical." I still believe that we dare not pursue our separate denominational goals as if our present divisions were not a scandal and a sin. I still believe that American church union of the kind proposed over four years ago is an obligation upon the members and leaders of our churches, challenging us all to a costly and risky seeking of the first step on the way toward reunion of the whole Church now.

These second thoughts consist, then, mainly of reflections upon

* On December 4, 1960, Dr. Blake preached a sermon in Grace Cathedral (Episcopal), San Francisco, entitled "A Proposal Toward the Reunion of Christ's Church." It was a call for the merger of four major Protestant denominations and led to the formation of the Consultation on Church Union, which is now engaged in developing plans for the merger of these and several other major denominations. Four years later Dr. Blake returned to the pulpit of Grace Cathedral and preached the following sermon. The text was: "Put on then as God's chosen ones, holy and beloved, compassion, kindness, lowliness, meekness and patience, forbearing one another and, if one has a complaint against another, forgiving each other; as the Lord has forgiven you, so you also must forgive. And above all these, put on love, which binds everything together in perfect harmony" (Colossians 3:12–14).

what has happened during these four years and of the developing insights from the gospel as to what Jesus Christ requires of any church which would bring its whole life under subjection to His Word.

Reflections on major events, 1961–1964. First let us recall the excited and widespread positive response inside and outside the churches which followed the concrete proposal of church union made in this pulpit now over four years ago and responded to so generously by the bishop of this diocese.

The mass media treated the proposal as a major news event and publicized it far beyond our cozy ecclesiastical circles. The secular response was overwhelmingly positive and cordial. The response in the denominations themselves was initially at least equally favorable. In my own Church nearly sixty presbyteries (out of two hundred) took separate initiatives to urge the General Assembly to issue the invitation that had been suggested. An invitation was issued in May, 1961, by that General Assembly, with hardly a dissenting voice, and was successively accepted by the four named churches, plus now two others which have joined officially in the Consultation on Church Union, which has met three times, once each spring, to "explore the establishment of a united church, truly catholic, truly reformed, and truly evangelical." To this consultation have come official observers from almost all the major Christian communions of the United States and Canada, including the Roman Catholic Church and the Standing Conference of Orthodox Bishops in North America.

This first result was welcome and not unexpected, but now, well after the event, I remind you that it could not have been taken for granted and certainly was not taken for granted by the preacher who made the proposal. When I stood here four years ago, I realized that without some such positive response my position and leadership in my own Church would have been greatly diminished.

The second event of major importance in these four years which bears upon the reunion of the Church has been the meeting of the second Vatican Council in Rome at the call of Pope John XXIII and continued by Pope Paul VI. It is fair to say that no one in all Christendom foresaw even the possibility of the contribution toward Christian unity that Vatican Council II would make, not only directly in relationship to all the non-Roman churches, but also by the amazing and miraculous renewal of the Roman Catholic Church itself. No Protestant dares ignore either the reality of Catholic renewal or its bearing upon the life and direction of all Christian churches. It is obvious that this event in some respects has made more important and urgent the effort to unite major Protestant churches and, in other respects, has forced a reassessment of the kind of union and cooperation that the new ecumenical climate now demands.

A third development in these four years which also bears upon Protestant reunion in North America is not so much a single event as it is a clear tendency upon the part of all churches to become more and more engaged in worldwide confessional relationships; that is, Anglicans everywhere are more and more interested in the other Anglican churches throughout the world, and Presbyterians in their fellow Presbyterian and Reformed churches. This is clearly true of the Anglican communion, the Lutheran churches, the Methodist Church, the Baptist bodies, and perhaps to a lesser extent, though clearly discernible, in the Presbyterian and Reformed World Alliance. This development, if it continues, will make any widespread reunion of Protestant and Anglican churches in North America less and less likely.

In the spring of 1963 the American churches became vitally involved in the racial crisis in this nation. As the national crisis in race relations developed, Christian churches, together with the Jewish communities, became deeply involved in action designed to purge themselves and the nation of racial injustice. This action program (as contrasted with earlier resolutions and pronouncements) has strained the unity of every Christian church so engaged. The possibility of new schisms, polarized on the one hand by the conviction that the life of American churches depended upon their moral commitment to racial justice and a wholly new pattern of race relations in church and nation and on the other hand by the conviction that such racial activities were beyond the churches' competence and mandate, threatening the very unity of the major denominations, had obviously an effect on church union discussions. This effect was ambiguous. For some it gave hope that church union could come by the moral renewal of the churches' relevance to real life. For others, it gave pause, wondering whether ecumenical and racial integration would divide parts of denominations from those in the same denominations who were "evangelical" and "conservative" in all social matters, including race.

Finally, it must be noted that, in addition to the lethargy which remains the greatest foe of any actual church unicn, there has developed in various quarters an actual hardening of opposition to church union proposals which may be expected to increase as the movement toward church union gives signs of strength or progress.

I have isolated these five developments of the past four years, some positive, some negative, and some ambiguɔus, to remind us here this morning that it is against such a background of events and developments that we must reassess both the urgency and possibility of church union in America in the full light of the gospel of Jesus Christ.

Because I continue to believe that the gospel of Jesus Christ lays a demand upon all churches that profess faith in Him, more fully to manifest the unity of the one Holy Catholic and Apostolic Church which is the gift of Jesus Christ by His Spirit, I call again upon my own Church—and in this particular pulpit, the Episcopal Church by name—plus any others in the United States and Canada, whether named in the sermon of four years ago or omitted, whether officially in the Consultation on Church Union or not, to find the way to take the first steps to unite our churches. This ought to be done now. Church union delayed is church union denied.

We must believe that if church union is according to the will of Christ, now is the time to get on with it. We dare not excuse ourselves, or abdicate our responsibility by leaving its accomplishment to the next generation or after so many years—a dozen or twenty-five or fifty—as some have suggested. I believe we ought to proceed with all seriousness now to solve the theological and organizational problems that prevent a union. If we are serious in our obedience, I have faith that Jesus Christ will illumine the way. There is no reason to believe that any later time will be a better time.

To this end, I suggest the necessary spirit of all such endeavor toward church union plus three specific warnings about dangers that must be avoided.

My text was chosen to remind us all, church leaders, ministers and priests, and lay members—for we are all equally involved and measurably responsible—of the right spirit church union will require. Let me read it to you again as the Apostle's word from God Himself and as it is applied to our spirit in seeking church union:

> Put on then as God's chosen ones, holy and beloved, compassion, kindness, lowliness, meekness and patience, forbearing one another and, if one has a complaint against another, forgiving each other; as the Lord has forgiven you, so you also must forgive. And above all these, put on love, which binds everything together in perfect harmony.

I cannot emphasize too strongly that no progress whatever may be expected in church union unless on the one hand we act in the conviction that we are a people chosen by God (set apart and beloved by Him) and on the other hand with a humility, a teachableness, a mutual forbearance, a willingness to forgive, and a Christian love which are not natural endowments, but a miraculous gift of grace.

It is in this spirit only that we dare to presume to find the will of Christ for our churches and, therefore, for all of us. And in a word I remind you that church union sought in this spirit will prevent any of us seeking a union in which others are asked to capitulate to our tradition. Furthermore, my text makes it abundantly clear that a united church reached by Christians so endued with the grace of God will be a renewed church and not a union of retreat produced either by profane motives or worldly events. To put dead churches together, to unite dying or faithless bodies, is not to produce a union in obedience to Jesus Christ.

In this spirit, then, let us remind ourselves of three pitfalls that ever threaten to trap those who would unite our churches.

1. We must be against any church union that is established at the expense of truth. It is because I believe we all need each other and can be enriched by the best of each other's faith and life that I press for church union now. A union produced by compromising convictions is not according to the will of Christ. This is the reason all of us must seek to understand and appreciate each other, and to forgive one another, much more than we usually do. A united church must fully confess the faith received by us

all from the ancient fathers and enriched by the insights of the separated fathers and contemporary brothers of our several traditions. The truth of Jesus Christ comprehends and transcends the faith of St. Augustine, St. Ignatius, and St. Francis. It includes the insights of Luther, Calvin, Hooker, Newman, Williams and Wesley. It embraces the Christian understanding of William Temple, Nathan Soderbloom, W. A. Visser 't Hooft, and Martin Luther King. The truth of Christ transcends them all and a united church must be built on no less comprehensive a base of Christian truth.

2. We must be against any church union that is motivated by, or aimed at, an outmoded triumphalism. I am indebted to Karl Rahner, the German Jesuit, more than to any other single writer, for making it clear to me in his book entitled *The Christian Commitment* how important it is for all Christian churches to give up, once and for all, the attitude, once almost universally held by them, that they ought to try to become powerful enough to dominate any state, society, or culture in which they are set. Those who still want the church, or churches, to dominate American life misread the signs of the times. The churches and their leaders must learn how to serve the world rather than to go on trying, as in the past, to rule it.

Rahner speaks to his Roman Catholic colleagues and through them to all of us as well:

> The loss of the church's medieval omnipotence in public life . . . was then theologically something to be expected, however much it may have involved guilt as well. The value given to the church in the public life of society, state, and culture in the Middle Ages cannot be regarded as something demanded by the very nature of the church. . . . The medieval form was possible only so long as the church was the church of a more or less closed culture. It became impossible from the moment when the West became an integral part of World History.

There are many Protestants, as there are Roman Catholics, who look back to the simpler past with a great nostalgia. They want their Church, as Church, to be dominant again as once it seemed to be. Some would argue for church union in the United States in order to make the Church more directly powerful again. This is as wrong as it is dangerous. We dare not conceive or work toward a church union in order to rule or dominate; we must seek church union in order to become better able to serve.

Perhaps the greatest single reason for anticlericalism in America today is the fear of the people (church members as well as others) that powerful churches, seeking tax support and tax exemption, will grow enough in strength to impose rigid uniformity of behavior upon the nation. This was James Madison's fear of the churches when our nation was founded. It is the common fear of all those who really know the history of the Christian Church in the West. It is not a pretty history.

I warn us all then that any church union motivated by a desire for increased wealth, efficiency, monopoly, or domination is a dangerous union and one that must be avoided.

3. Finally, we must be against any church union that would in any way threaten the Ecumenical Movement or diminish the obligation to continue to cooperate with all Christian churches in their common witness to the Lordship of Jesus Christ.

I remind you that were the contemplated church union, as presently envisaged, completed next year, there still would be major Christian churches in this country and all over the world with which such a united church would be under obligation to cooperate in common witness and service to the world. The largest of these is the Roman Catholic Church. We dare not, in loyalty to Jesus Christ, make rigid a polemical Protestantism against that Church. We are only now beginning to understand what possibilities are before us for common Catholic and Protestant work and witness. But in addition, there will remain the Eastern Orthodox churches, requiring much more patient understanding than we Westerners usually show toward them. I merely list the other major groups of churches with which we are obliged to continue and increase ecumenical cooperation: the Lutheran bodies, the Baptist churches, the remaining Reformed and Presbyterian churches, and finally, the wide range of self-styled "evangelical" churches and Pentecostals which, in our pride, we usually call sects.

I hope my point is clear. Church union must never be thought of as a substitute for, or an alternative to, ecumenical cooperation of all Christian churches. The kind of church union which alone we dare to press for is one which is recognized clearly as supplementary to all other manifestations of Christian unity, especially those obligations laid upon us all by the new ecumenical insights of the twentieth century.

I have just returned from eastern Nigeria, where the Central Committee of the World Council of Churches has met for the first time on the continent of Africa. A church gathering on that continent is forced to consider church union in the light of the great and unfinished tasks of mission and evangelism there, as well as in the light of the necessity for Western churches to be purged and purified of their cultural involvement with colonialism and race prejudice.

And so today I say to you:

Led, I pray by the Holy Spirit, I propose that we press on in North America to form, with all who will join with us, "a united church, truly catholic, truly reformed, and truly evangelical," lest in this revolutionary world we find ourselves so bound to our own past histories that we are unable to be God's instrument for peace and reconciliation across all boundaries of nation, race, or class. And I call upon you to seek this union in the only spirit which Jesus Christ can bless as expressed by the Apostle in my text:

> Put on then as God's chosen ones, holy and beloved, compassion, kindness, lowliness, meekness and patience, forbearing one another and, if one has a complaint against another, forgiving each other; as the Lord has forgiven you, so you also must forgive. And above all these, put on love, which binds everything together in perfect harmony.

Chapter 21

SOME IMPLICATIONS OF
A UNITED CHURCH*

I SUPPOSE that a major implication of a *united* church, evangelical, catholic, and reformed, is that there is enough wrong with our present *divided* state that the effort to unite a number of our present denominations is worthwhile.

This is apparently something which cannot be taken for granted even though it has long been ecclesiastically fashionable to confess the scandal of division and to intercede for the visible unity of Christ's Church. There is a surprising reluctance, quite widespread, to draw any practical or realistic conclusions from the theological consensus, which exists, as to the true nature of the Church.

I have been sometimes tempted to think that one could say that all those who are dissatisfied with the present state and mission of the Church in the United States of America would also be *for* church union and that only those quite complacent about how we are doing would be *against* it. But that is only partly true. It is true that the complacent churchmen are against church union, but I am convinced that there are a great many churchmen and theologians who are quite radical in their criticism of the church "as is" who nevertheless are quite apathetic about church union.

It is to that group that I address myself. The implications of a united church, evangelical, catholic, and reformed, to which I shall draw your attention are those which I hope will stimulate some of you to begin to support church union who until now have evidenced little interest in it, much less active and enthusiastic support for it.

I shall take it for granted that you are as much concerned as I that the Church in the United States in 1965 is, by and large, weak in its witness to the gospel, irrelevant to the major concerns

* This address was delivered in 1965.

of most people, and singularly mute or muffled when it tries to sound a clarion call to follow Jesus Christ in individual or social commitment. We still do pretty well in organizational statistics and from time to time, and place to place, there is life and power evidenced in race relations or other social interests. But I shall not take time to try to persuade you that the church needs renewal and a sharper focus of its mission. Rather, I shall try by what I say to persuade any of you who need that persuasion that church union is important both to renewal and to the fulfillment of mission.

Here, then, is my series of implications:

1. *To produce a united church, evangelical, catholic, and reformed, is not essentially an organizational matter.*

I suppose it is partly because my own work is that of church administration that it is difficult for "anti-institutional" theologians and "anti-institutional" theological students to believe I could possibly have a concern that transcended the church as institution.

I freely admit that I am interested in church, as institution and organization, and that I have difficulty even in understanding some of you when you write or speak as if the institution were not worth saving. But I do insist that I take some of your theological analyses and conclusions about the church more seriously than you apparently do.

The ecumenical theology that is now being formed all over the world in such institutions as this emphasizes the corporate unity of the "people of God," the Body of Christ. This biblically based interest in ecclesiology makes it perfectly clear that denominations, as we have known them and as we continue to take them for granted, have no theological base whatever. Church, meaning *una sancta,* is a biblical concept. Church, meaning a gathering of people in a community or a part of a community (meeting even in somebody's house), is a proper use of the word. But to call any denomination "church" is theologically indefensible even though practically inevitable in our divided state. Denominationalism, as such, distorts our understanding of the gospel, cripples the effectiveness of our witness, and encourages "culture religion" in the place of Christianity.

When, therefore, one begins to work toward the establishment of a united church, evangelical, catholic, and reformed, it is not basically an organizational task at all, although a plan of union must include organization, but rather a theological task. If we could only get our theological assumptions right, the organizational conclusions would pretty well take care of themselves.

2. *A united church, evangelical, catholic, and reformed, implies neither uniformity, ecclesiastical capitulation, nor theological dilution, but rather seeks a union of mutual enrichment.*

One of the great fears of all Protestants, which naturally arises from their early history vis-à-vis Rome, is that of imposed uniformity. The famous woman who threw her stool at a bishop in St. Giles Kirk in Edinburgh, not because he was a bishop (bad enough), but because he was imposing an unwanted liturgy upon the congregation, is a continuing symbol of Protestant resistance to imposed uniformity.

But such a church union as is being proposed does not even imply uniformity, let alone imposed uniformity. Even the Roman Catholic Church with all its authoritarian prelacy has not produced uniformity although there is less liturgical and other kinds of chaos in that Church than in most Protestant churches. Freedom we want but do we want chaos? The near bankruptcy of much Protestant worship indicates the need of a common understanding of what worship is. It does not imply either uniform practice or a single liturgy. It was a wise member of the Consultation on Church Union who noted that divided Protestantism is rapidly producing churches more and more uniform in their attempt to compete for the support of the middle-class person by doing whatever that person considers the fashion. The same man suggested that a united church might very well be the only way to insure a variety of service and program that might appeal more broadly to the needs and tastes of men.

A second fear of church union quite widespread is that it implies a "sell-out" of our tradition. Personally I am not interested in a united church that is produced by the capitulation of any tradition to another. The interesting thing is that any good plan of union is always judged by partisans to be a capitulation.

But such partisan judgments cancel each other out. In fact one good way to decide whether a plan is in fact a good one is to be sure that the barrage of criticism is generally equal from all directions—contrary to the politician who said: "I can tell the people are behind me from the direction of the rocks."

Let me illustrate this point concretely. It is presently proposed

that there be bishops in this united church. In fact, I proposed it
five years ago in the sermon in Grace Cathedral. I have been
accused of selling out my Presbyterian tradition. But my reasons
for proposing that there be bishops were that non-Episcopal
churches, including my own, either already have officials who are
sometimes worse than bishops, whatever we call them, or are
coming to the conclusion that they need the kind of pastoral and
symbolic office that bishops at their best are or always have been.
I had another chief reason also. Episcopacy is present in most
Christian churches throughout the world. Ultimate unity can practically be achieved or contemplated only as a constitutional and
chastened episcopacy.

A third fear of church union is that it implies the sacrifice of
truth by comparison—the watering down of theological conviction replaced by an immoral tolerance.

Those of us who presently represent the six churches in the
Consultation fully recognize this as a danger, but we are committed to a radically different way to achieve union. We are convinced that we will get nowhere by a compromise procedure, for
example, "You Anglicans can have bishops but we Congregationalists will balance that by retaining absolute independency of
the congregations, and we will let the Presbyterians have their
ruling elders."

Or to illustrate more theologically, we are convinced that although there are real and important theological cleavages in
American churches, these cleavages do not generally follow denominational lines, but rather cut right across them. The only
hope is that there is or will be enough biblical and theological
renewal to enable our churches to grasp together a new and richer
theological understanding of the gospel for our own day and
place.

The union that we seek and believe is God's will for his Church
is one of mutual enrichment. Let me illustrate what I mean in an
area where there is a maximum of mutual suspicion, namely,
priesthood and Eucharist.

Last year the Consultation on Church Union met in Lexington,
Kentucky. The common Communion service, a feature of each
meeting, was held under the authority of the Christian Churches
(Disciples) at the historic Cove Ridge Meeting House not far
from Lexington. This building was originally a Presbyterian

church, but that ecclesiastical embarrassment is beside the point I wish to make.

My point is that theologically one would take for granted that the Anglo-Catholics' and the Disciples' points of view on ministry and Sacrament would be at the extremes of the theological spectrum represented in the Consultation. The latter, for example, by conviction and tradition have laymen administer the Sacrament. They are not even in the argument whether we non-Episcopally ordained ministers can administer a Sacrament valid in Anglo-Catholic tradition.

But being in that service together made more of us realize for the first time that the chief reason for the Disciples' tradition and practice was because, like the Anglo-Catholics, they believed that the frequent and regular celebration of the Sacrament was essential to Christian worship. I am not now at liberty to describe the details of what may be a most important theological breakthrough based upon this insight, which has been discussed by a special commission of the Consultation, but I can say that here, as at least at one other difficult theological place, we were all excited at the new light that apparently was coming to us from the Holy Spirit.

What I am saying is that this is a far different thing from theological compromise to produce a lowest common denominator faith. Is it possible that church union is the only way the American churches can get a fuller and richer grasp of truth? Is it possible that church division complacently accepted is the surest way to sacrifice and distort the truth that comes from God?

3. *A united church, evangelical, catholic, and reformed, does not imply a diversion of attention from the prophetic mission of the Church in and to the world, but may be God's way of enabling us to fulfill it.*

The most troubling criticisms of the proposal for church union are that it was proposed to produce an upper-middle-class Protestant Church and that the inevitable result of the effort would be to turn these denominations in upon themselves at the very moment when they should be losing themselves in a sacrificial mission in and to the world.

Let me respond to the first part of that criticism with a fact. One of the great Negro denominations has officially decided to enter the Consultation as a full participant and two others are likely to join as well. This united church aims at full catholicity in this sense of being more fully inclusive, racially, economically, socially, and ethnically than any of the present denominations.

But what do we say to those who charge we are fiddling ecclesiastically while Rome burns?

I think most of you would agree that I have the right to speak of the Church's involvement in the struggle for racial freedom, equality, and justice in these past three years. Let me put it flatly this way: If I had not been for church union before becoming fully involved in the churches' effort to be rightly involved in the civil rights movement, my experience in trying to mobilize the troops of Jesus Christ for this engagement would have converted me to church union. Nothing, in my considered opinion, stands so much in the way of the churches' proper involvement and witness in the world than the present denominational division of the Church.

To seek church union and to seek prophetic witness are not contradictory or mutually exclusive choices for an American Christian in 1965. They demand and imply each other; you cannot fully do either without the other; they both stem from the same theological understanding of what the Church is.

In conclusion, let me mention briefly two other fears of church union widely present even if not always expressed.

There is the fear of bigness, and I share that fear. But I know that bigness is upon us whether we have church union or not. Do you believe the Methodist Church has no problems of bigness? Or the Presbyterian? But what is the alternative? To remain small, intimate religious clubs or fraternities with a closed membership? What would that do to evangelistic zeal?

We live in a time of great nostalgia for the passing intimacies of a rural culture that is already gone. Big government, big business, big unions, big political parties, big cities are the environment of our life. The best way to insure increasing irrelevance of the Church in the United States is to let our common fear of bigness and our common nostalgia for the simpler past be our excuses for perpetuating the denominations as they exist and to do it in the mistaken idea that a church of one million members is really more intimate than one of twenty million.

Finally there is the fear of monopoly. Scandinavia and Greece are pointed to as horrible examples of religious monopoly. To discuss this question responsibly would require another address almost as long as this one. Therefore, let me remind you that nothing in the present proposal remotely presages anything resembling religious monopoly. If the Consultation on Church Union succeeds, as I continue to pray it will, there still would be in the United States, in addition to it, the Roman Catholic Church, the Orthodox and Lutheran churches, as well as many so-called free churches, such as the Baptist, the Pentecostals, and the Friends. I am suggesting that the discussion of religious monopoly can safely be put off until a later occasion.

The Consultation on Church Union is busy at its work. We hope we soon will be writing a definite plan of union. Then we pray for a miracle not unlike that which we have seen in our time wrought by God through his charismatic servant, Pope John XXIII. Nothing less will enable us to be obedient to Jesus Christ in our day and place.

Chapter 22

MOTIVES FOR CHURCH UNION *

I SHALL concentrate on a single aspect of American church union which I judge to be crucial to the actual achievement of an organic union in our time, namely, motives.

I speak of motives for American church union because I believe that unless our motives in seeking church union are made clear, strengthened, and more widely accepted, there will be no union in our time.

Let me list four reasons for American church union which I do judge to be right, central, and major. These reasons, if accepted by the ministers and members of our churches, would become motives sufficiently powerful to produce in our time an American church union which in fact would be an important first step toward the reunion of Christ's Church in all the world.

1. The six American churches of the Consultation on Church Union should seek to establish "a united church, truly catholic, truly reformed, and truly evangelical" because *obedience to Jesus Christ* requires it. I am conscious of the fact that if I could establish this reason in the minds and hearts of church members, no other reason would be required to motivate a church union. I also know that such a reason so stated can be misunderstood as implying that everyone who is against this particular church union is, therefore, disobedient to the Lord Jesus Christ. This I do not mean to imply.

But—let me emphasize it—I do believe that anything less than the conviction that Jesus Christ requires a church union will be insufficient as a motive to achieve it against the obstacles that stand in the way. The other three reasons that I shall list are in

* The following address was given to the Newman Foundation of Kansas City, Missouri, on May 28, 1964.

a sense arguments that this American church union is according to the will of Christ. But here let me examine the necessity of a motivation that is basically spiritual and tied in with the essential motivation of a Christian to obey the revealed will of Jesus Christ.

Since it is easier for all of us to take for granted the divided Church, we must be moved by Jesus Christ Himself if we are to press for a manifest unity of Christ's disciples, a unity which will require all of us to repent the past and to seek His will anew. Lethargy, convenience, selfishness, human limitation, fear, historical memories, and our present loyalties all work against striving for church union. Only the belief that we ought to unite will be sufficient to overcome the reasons against a particular church union.

Prayer to God that we may be obedient to Him as He is revealed in our Lord Jesus Christ is the only foundation upon which a united church may be established: prayer that we may have sufficient courage, wisdom, and love to be radically obedient to our common Lord; prayer that requires us to be willing to give up our cherished particularities in order to receive new gifts from our Lord Himself; prayer that we may be Christ's agents of reconciliation among His disciples and in the world—this kind of prayer alone will produce the right and effective motive for church union.

2. These six American churches should seek to establish "a united church truly catholic, truly reformed, and truly evangelical" because such a union would enable them to challenge the world to respond to the gospel at home and abroad with an effectiveness impossible in their separateness.

Those of us who are inside these six churches have no true understanding of the spectacle we exhibit to the very people outside the Church whom we presumably wish to persuade to become Christians with us. To them we look like a group of competing religious clubs, more often behaving like Greek-letter fraternities in a college than like the bride or body of Jesus Christ, which we all claim the Church to be. Such a spectacle makes our preaching sound like biased propaganda and reduces the Lord's Supper to agnostic ritual for initiates.

The increasing urbanization of American life and the accompanying necessity for mass communication to masses of city dwellers make effective evangelism almost impossible today. Tomorrow will be worse. The result of continuing division and competition for members and support will but produce twenty-five "culture churches" in an increasingly secular society. The churches themselves will ultimately suffer the fate of the Masonic Order and the Knights of Columbus, becoming relics of a religious history quite irrelevant to the issues of life and death. Baptism, whether infants' or believers', will degenerate further into an initiatory rite marking one's religious family inheritance. The erosion of the generations will produce a larger and larger percentage of secularists, both outside and inside the membership of the churches.

Since in separation it will be important organizationally for each separate church to conserve, if not enlarge, its constituency, ethical and spiritual requirements for membership will progressively be reduced and discipline of membership will disappear.

I do not need to be a prophet to make such predictions. It is happening now. If it were not for the mobility of the American people and the constantly increasing marriages across religious lines, we would already have reached the state of finally fixed religious culture communities, living side by side in all our cities and suburbs. The end result of such a religious pattern is religious communalism, such as you have in Lebanon, India, and in much of Europe.

The present division of the Church of Jesus Christ into twenty-five major denominations is making true evangelism—that is, the winning of converts to the one Lord Jesus Christ—an increasingly difficult undertaking. Church statistics indicate that plateaus have been reached of these culture members. One can be glad that it is impossible to reflect in statistics the number of true conversions to the Lord Jesus Christ, for if that were possible, the desperate weakness of churches in the United States would be revealed.

Look also for a moment at the effect of our present divisions in Christian evangelism overseas. Fifty years ago and more, our ablest missionaries were reporting that the gospel was being obscured by the divisions, theological and cultural, which we were exporting from America with our missionaries. Bishop Brent of the Protestant Episcopal Church was one of those who saw the problem first and most clearly. The faith and order movement arose from his concern.

To date, one church union of true ecumenical significance has been achieved, that of South India. Efforts to emulate that union are, in various stages of development, being made all over Africa and Asia. But it is evident that unless more real help, not only by precept, but by example, is given by Christians in the United States and Europe, these union efforts either will fail or will be built on anti-Western nationalism. The survival of a small minority of Christians in Asia and Africa depends upon unity and union. How much more evident is it that church divisions make evangelism ineffective in such lands.

My second reason then for the importance of American church union now is that without it we may be sure that evangelism is and will be greatly hindered. It should be understood that I have not said that American church union would so renew the Church that the gospel would be surely heard and heeded by the world. But surely what I have said about the barrier to evangelism created by our disunity makes a powerful motive toward church union.

3. These six American churches should seek to establish "a united church truly catholic, truly reformed, and truly evangelical" because such a union would greatly strengthen the ethical witness of Christianity in American life. I have said several times since last summer that if I had not been for church union before the civil rights crisis faced the nation, I would be for church union now. I shall not take the time to describe the hindrances and frustrations occasioned by our divisions as we have attempted in these past twelve months to mobilize Christian forces in this effort to establish freedom, justice, and equality for all Americans. Will you take it on the authority of one who has been so involved on the national level that it is no easier there than on the local level to bring to bear the moral force of our churches upon this or any ethical problem?

With regard to race, we do have the advantage that the separate churches basically agree on what is right and what is wrong. Ten years ago when the churches were fighting McCarthyism and twenty-five years ago when they were fighting Coughlinism, we had the spectacle of the churches seriously divided on public and political matters. When Father Coughlin was embarrassing Roman Catholics twenty-five years ago, I confess that most Protestants rather enjoyed the fun. And I suspect that Roman Catholics felt something the same when Senator McCarthy was getting a brief hearing for his false and vicious charges that the Protestant clergy had been infiltrated by communists.

Thank God that those times are past. Today both Protestants

and Roman Catholics realize that an attack against the other hurts both, for however you explain it theologically, Jesus Christ is somehow represented by all the churches that bear His name.

The progress that has been made in racial relations in the past twelve months, slight though it is in relationship to that required for justice, has been greatly forwarded by the unity of action of the churches. I refer you to the comments made by the Attorney General and by many congressional leaders as authority for my statement. But we would have done much better had we not been divided into so many separate communions.

Or, look to another politico-moral issue faced by the United States and the whole world—that of peace. If Christianity is to make its contribution to the saving of the world from nuclear self-destruction, it will be vital that the Church of Jesus Christ speak with one voice. The difficulty of speaking with that voice is that we are in fact many voices. Again, I do not say that this American church union will assure a clear and effective moral witness by the Church, but I do say that, divided as we are, we are less effective than we ought to be in questions of race, peace, family life, delinquency, crime, gambling, sexual deviation, and materialism—you name the problem!

4. Finally, these six American churches should seek to establish "a united church truly catholic. truly reformed, and truly evangelical" because such a union would enrich each of the churches and remove from them some of the distortions caused by the divisions among them. One of the strongest reasons offered against church union is indicated by the common question: "What do we have to give up?" The strongest motive for church union will be developed when that question is replaced by: "What enrichment may we expect to receive in a union with these other Christian Churches?"

However loyal each of us is to the particular Christian tradition in which he finds himself, he ought to be impressed by now that other traditions contain treasures of faith and life which could enrich his Church. This is the result of the Ecumenical Movement. When our churches were in the process of dividing, their theologians had of necessity to argue polemically against the aberrations of the others. Such arguments distorted each of the traditions. One reason why Catholic preaching has for four hundred years been neglected is that Protestants preached. One reason that the Lord's

Supper has been pushed out of the center of Protestant worship is that the Mass was the center of Catholic devotion. One reason that Catholic Communion tended to become magical was that Protestant Communion had become subjectivistic. One could go on and on listing the distortions large and small that our divisions have produced.

The positive point I would make is that church union—the only kind in which I am interested—can recapture for us all the fullness of Christian faith and life. I have said elsewhere, and I repeat it because I believe it is so crucial, that the Ecumenical Movement has produced an atmosphere in which it is now possible for us to find to our surprise that the very practice or article of belief we had been taught was wrong in another tradition may in fact be an emphasis, the lack of which is our own Church's chief problem. It was not until I had listened to Orthodox theologians for some years that it finally came home to me how much my own Church needed the continuity with all the past, the joy in the Eucharist, and the transcendence of the culture that are common in Orthodoxy. And may I be forgiven if I suggest that Christians of Catholic tradition may find in Protestant tradition and biblical faith enrichments that they need as much.

No church union can be contemplated as anything other than a betrayal of truth by those who believe that their Church has nothing to learn from the other churches. The strongest motive for church union is established when Christian men, in obedience to Jesus Christ, come to the realization that their separate existences in separate churches is an impoverishment of them all.

My hope for American church union is based ultimately on the conviction that Christ requires it. Obedience to that One Jesus Christ alone will make Christians one.

Chapter 23

TOLERANCE VERSUS FAITH*

IN a pluralistic society where all kinds of people must learn to live together, even when they basically disagree about many things, tolerance becomes an essential virtue. In our country there are Christians and Jews; there are humanists and agnostics; there are libertines and pietists. Somehow we must all live together in peace. In order for us to live together in any decent way there must be a measure of tolerance by all for all.

In the world as a whole the problem of coexistence with others is even more complicated. For in addition to the major groups we find in our own pluralistic society, we are confronted in the world with Hindus and Buddhists, Mohammedans, and atheists in large and self-conscious groupings. Convinced communists, militant fascists, racists, nationalists, revolutionaries, and conservatives all have their differing convictions. Asians, Africans, and Latin Americans do not have the same faith or make the same assumptions as North Americans or Europeans. The problem of peace and even of survival appears to depend in the long range upon all these groups of people developing enough tolerance of each other's convictions to coexist in a measure of peace and tranquility.

It is not surprising, then, to note how public officials at all levels, whether mayors, governors, presidents, or the Secretary General of the United Nations, continually urge tolerance upon all parties to potential disputes. Civil order and world peace appear to depend most upon tolerant self-restraint.

But a man of faith, or of any deep conviction, feels that he

---

* The following sermon was delivered in 1965 and has as its text: " 'And there is salvation in no one else, for there is no other name under heaven given among men by which we must be saved' " (Acts 4:12).

must, to be a man, stand for that in which he believes. So the white mayor of a Mississippi town believes he cannot tolerate the breaking of law by civil rights demonstrators any more than those demonstrators are willing longer to tolerate the injustices that custom and law continue to impose upon them.

Most Americans feel that our democratic traditions of freedom and justice under law are of such fundamental importance to all men that, with our power and responsibility, we must be intolerant of revolutionary communism and resist its spread and undermine its success and influence everywhere. Equally it appears that the leaders of the People's Republic of China are convinced that they must destroy what they call our "imperialism"; they are unwilling to try to coexist with us and refuse even to discuss our points of difference or conflict. And between these extremes is the whole galaxy of less powerful nations and peoples who hope and pray that the conflict building up between the big powers will not destroy them all, along with us.

But I mention this great problem of political and ideological conflict, as I did the civil rights conflict, not in the hope of solving it in a sermon, but as an illustration of the moral and spiritual issue with which all men ought to be concerned, namely, the conflict in all of us between tolerance and conviction or faith.

This is not a new conflict. It is as old as human history. To look at it, let us examine the familiar incident in Jerusalem at the very beginning of the Christian Era when Peter and John found themselves in conflict with the rulers of their city and nation.

Peter and John were the acknowledged leaders of a rapidly growing company of people who were followers of the crucified and risen Jesus of Nazareth, whom they believed to be the long-awaited Messiah. Since the religious authorities in Jerusalem had instigated and supported the execution of Jesus by the Roman authorities in order to stop what they feared was a revolutionary movement against both Church and State, it is clear that Peter's bold public preaching of the risen Lord had to be stopped if their authority with the people was not to be completely undermined.

Added to Peter's eloquence was the wonder of the healing of a lame man, well known in the city. The miracle seemed to the people to authenticate Peter's claims about Jesus of Nazareth. And Peter himself spoke publicly, indicating that it was by the name and power of Jesus that the healing of the lame man had been accomplished.

This was too much for the authorities. It was evening, so they arrested Peter and John and kept them in custody overnight. Next day the high priest and the elders of the people called the two apostles before them and asked them by what power or authority they had healed the man.

Peter did not hesitate or quibble, but eloquently replied: "Rulers of the people and elders, if we are being examined today concerning a good deed done to a cripple, by what means this man has been healed, be it known to you all, and to all the people of Israel, that by the name of Jesus Christ of Nazareth, whom you crucified, whom God raised from the dead, by him this man is standing before you well."

And then to make the confrontation entirely clear, he continued speaking of Jesus: "This is the stone which was rejected by you builders, but which has become the head of the corner. And there is salvation in no one else, for there is no other name under heaven given among men by which we must be saved."

In the face of the Apostles' conviction and boldness in stating it, the authorities were forced, because of the support of the people, to let the apostles go merely with a warning. Peter and John returned to their supporters. The Christian Church was thus launched on its worldwide mission, based upon the conviction and the faith so boldly and unequivocally stated by Peter in my text.

The question is whether we Christians still have this faith. It is not an easy conviction to hold on to, or to live by, that Jesus Christ is the only hope of the salvation of men. To the modern rational man it sounds like a pretentious claim by us Christians, a sort of hangover from the day, long since past, when Christendom was a reality and Christian ideas and Christian power were without any real rival for world domination.

This summer I heard an address by the Secretary General of the United Nations, U Thant, before an international audience in Europe, the thesis of which was very simple and apparently acceptable to his hearers. I remind you that U Thant is a Buddhist. In effect he said that a few centuries ago religious tolerance was generally considered a sin or a crime. Christians and Mohammedans both believed that they were doing God's will if they tried by any means, including violence, to impose their faith upon the other. Catholics and Protestants were equally intolerant of the other's interpretation of the Christian faith. "But now," said the Secretary General of the United Nations, "in the new spirit of the ecumenical movement, it is widely recognized that tolerance of differences in religious conviction is a virtue and not a sin or crime."

He went on to express his hope and belief that soon men would come to the same tolerant attitude toward political and economic ideology. Today in Moscow and Peking, it is a crime and a Marxist "sin" to be tolerant of capitalism and traditional political democracy. Equally in London and Washington, it is treason to adopt the communist answers to the political and economic problems of our world. U Thant suggested that so long as the Chinese and Russians based their policy simply on the destruction of "imperialism" and so long as the United States based its policy on simple anticommunism, the world would teeter on the edge of nuclear destruction. He lay his hope for peace on an increase of tolerance on both sides of the world ideological conflict.

I came away from the address considerably troubled. I recognized, as do most rational men, that there was much truth in what he said. History is full of illustrations of men and nations creating horror and violence by their intransigent convictions, whether religious or political.

Nevertheless, I am troubled by this common, liberal rational and secular solution to the salvation of the world, for two reasons:

Is it really true that political peace will come in our time only if the protagonists give up their convictions and become tolerant of each other?

Is it a right reading of what has happened in the realm of religion in this ecumenical age, namely, that men no longer have specific faith enough that they are now willing to substitute tolerance for conviction? Let us examine these two questions.

Let me not be misunderstood in my answer to the first question. I am sure that the attitude of our radical right and the matching attitude of Peking are both wrong. And they are wrong for the same reason. Both make the mistake, or commit the sin, if you will, of identifying their limited position with truth spelled with a capital "T," as if any man were God. The only political hope of peace in our world is not simply giving up conviction to replace it with amoral tolerance, but rather in finding a humbler and more understanding way of holding on to our convictions. The reason that United States foreign policy is so widely unpopular, even in the neutralist bloc of nations today, is not because justice, freedom, respect for the individual, and traditional democracy are being repudiated by the peoples of the world, but rather because in our actual policy we seem to most others to be using these ideals of the American Revolution as a smoke screen to hide our willingness to do almost anything to protect our wealth and power against the poor and the colored peoples of the world.

The American contribution to the peace of the world will not come from a lazy immoral tolerance for the evils of communist totalitarianism. Rather our contribution to the peace of the world will come in the measure by which we recapture in our time the political faith and practice that made our nation great and our history glorious. The greatest enemy of the true American revolution is not centered in Peking or Moscow, it is centered in the hearts and minds of all of us who are willing to let our wealth, our power, our fears, or our white supremacy betray the best ideals of Washington, Jefferson, Jackson, and Abraham Lincoln. And we will not even realize how our policy and stance appear, both to our friends and enemies, unless we are willing to listen to and to heed their criticisms of our way of life. How any American can be so sure that our present way of life is the economic and political solution for the whole world, as most of us seem to be, seems fantastic in the wake of the eruptions we have witnessed in Los Angeles and Chicago—eruptions that are the surface indications of the deep and festering disease in our own body politic.

On the other hand, it is equally clear that so long as communist leaders are unwilling to see and recognize their own corruptions of their communist ideal, they will make no real contribution either to their own socialist dream or to world peace.

Let me then repeat and sum up. The hope of world peace does not depend on an immoral giving up of anyone's faith or conviction in favor of an amoral tolerance. It depends rather on men devoting themselves, unselfishly, to the best virtues and ideals they profess to serve. The source of evil is not faith, it is sin, selfishness, and hypocrisy.

Is my second question a right reading of what has happened in the realm of religion in this ecumenical age, namely, that men no longer have specific faith enough that they are now willing to substitute tolerance for conviction?

This is the most common misunderstanding of the Ecumenical Movement, both among its friends and among its critics. I find to my horror that despite anything I say most Christians seem to suppose that I am preaching a watered-down gospel that almost any rational man of good will, with a Christian bias or prejudice, can accept.

While it is true that ecumenical leaders in the churches are all urging their members to break out of the narrow limits of their denominational traditions and accept with joy the truth that other Christian traditions have cherished and preserved, it is a complete misunderstanding of the Ecumenical Movement to suppose that it would sacrifice truth for tolerance or substitute some wishy-washy compromise for the apostolic faith in Jesus Christ of the one holy Catholic Church.

The source of the power of the Ecumenical Movement in the Church and in the world today rises out of its recapturing in purer and more pristine form that faith in Jesus of Nazareth that Peter proclaimed so boldly when, under pressure from the government and culture of his nation, he said: "There is salvation in no one else, for there is no other name under heaven given among men by which we must be saved."

The ecumenical faith that is being pressed upon all Christian people during these revolutionary days is not an easy faith consisting of multicultural good will and tolerance. It is a faith in Jesus Christ, the Son of God, the Savior of the world—a faith that is under all the cultural pressure it ever has been in the twenty centuries of its existence. Again and again this central affirmation of Christianity has been obscured by limiting cultural accretions; again and again it has been betrayed by men who used its formulae to cover up their hate, their fears, or their hypocrisies. But thanks be to God, there are signs in the life of every church that God's Holy Spirit is moving among His people, not only to help them understand and reformulate what is essential Christian faith, but also in courage to witness boldly for it by their acts of service, healing, and love for all men.

The fruit of this Holy Spirit remains what it always has been in the lives of all the saints: "Love, joy, peace, patience, kindness, goodness, faithfulness, gentleness, self-control."

The recapturing of these marks of faith is the number one task and duty of each company of God's people in every congregation in every nation of the world. These gifts (for they are gifts from God—we cannot create them in ourselves) rise out of the grace of God through faith in Jesus Christ.

This understanding of faith is a very different thing from the intolerant or hypocritical imposition of our religious ideology upon other men. It is rather the humble response of men like the first Christians to the love and power of God in Jesus Christ which enabled Peter and John to say to those who pressed them to betray their Lord by silence: "Whether it is right in the sight of God to listen to you rather than to God, you must judge, for we cannot but speak of what we have seen and heard."

Chapter 24

THE CHURCH IN THE
NEXT DECADE *

TEN years in the life of the Church is hardly long enough to measure the ebb and flow of the tides of its history. It is too easy in such a short span to mistake a surface squall for the wave of the future. Nevertheless, the world and the Church are changing rapidly enough these days to make even half-decades significant. Who, writing in January, 1961, would have guessed at the profound adjustments we would witness in the Roman Catholic Church in just five years?

Let us look then at the immediate prospect of the Church as we approach the end of the third quarter of the twentieth century. In this article I will not attempt to prophesy as to this future but rather to analyze the pressures in and on the Church, and to suggest what we ought, therefore, to aim at and to pray for.

For the first time in a generation, theological unrest appears to be developing with regard to the ecumenical consensus that has been the influential movement of thought for a whole generation and more in the United States. Karl Barth started the dominant theology of the past generation. Reinhold Niebuhr translated it into the American idiom. Insofar as American churchmen have been theologically influenced, we have been moved by this consensus, whether our beginnings were "fundamentalist" or "modernist," to use the labels of the teens and twenties.

The chief points of this ecumenical theology are four: (1) a transcendent God, who has revealed Himself in Jesus Christ; (2) knowledge of this God found in a historical reading and under-

---

* The following article was written for the twenty-fifth anniversary issue of the journal *Christianity and Crisis*, February 21, 1966.

standing of the Scriptures; (3) a recapturing of the heart of orthodox beliefs in creation, salvation, and eschatology; and (4) a radical challenge to the ethics that most Christians had taken for granted for several centuries.

The chief weakness of this position was its tendency toward a narrow biblicism, which threatened its ability to communicate with a world that does not take the Scriptures seriously, and its lack of a metaphysics, cutting off the theologians of the Church from any fruitful dialogue with the philosophers.

Tillich began responsbily to challenge point one metaphysically and thereby to raise questions about point three. The present fad of "death of God" theology is a shallow treatment of the same important theme. Bultmann and his successors raise fundamental questions about point two. And as churches have attempted to implement point four, they find that their members generally equate the new ethics with the secularist relativism that threatens all they have believed. My guess is that the main influence of theology within our churches in the next decade will continue to be the ecumenical consensus, refined but not fundamentally challenged.

This judgment is reinforced by the amazing renewal of the Roman Catholic Church, a renewal essentially, though somewhat belatedly, based upon the ecumenical theology described above. The second internal pressure for change upon the Protestant and Orthodox churches, their leaders, and people arises out of this Catholic renewal. Whatever one's optimism or pessimism, however much or little one trusts the motives of ecumenical Catholics, there is a new factor here that must be seriously reckoned with.

The next ten years will be marked by all kinds of responses to the Roman Catholic entrance into the life of the Ecumenical Movement. The influence of the Church of Rome will generally be to reinforce each of the four points of the ecumenical theology since orthodox dogma is not challenged in that Church, and, for-tunately, the most profound changes arising out of Vatican II would appear to be those of increased reliance upon the Scriptures (historically interpreted) and a radical reassessment of the ethical responsibilities of the Church in the modern world.

A third internal pressure upon all the churches is the new place of the laity in the life of the Church. Sometimes it looks like nothing but a new anticlericalism, which threatens the peace and unity of Protestant leaders and ministers as much as it does the Catholic hierarchy and priests. But the bright side of this movement is that the minister or priest conceived of as the hired professional Christian is clearly on the way out.

The hope of every church will be to find the way to let the laity minister in the Church and in the world. Whether the increased influence and participation of lay Christians will be positive or negative is the crucial question. It is coming, willy-nilly. The effect may be tragedy, unless the lay movement is truly and firmly grounded in the gospel.

Finally, perhaps the most important internal pressure upon the churches stems from the confusion and frustration of the local pastor. It has been described in many ways. Some see in the flight from the pastorate merely a symptom of anti-institutionalism in the younger generation. Others see in it the obvious result of lay resistance to any leadership that would change the congregation from its nineteenth-century pattern, in which all the powerful lay members grew up and of which they still nostalgically approve.

In my judgment there is a deeper cause than either of these. Too many pastors have failed to find any real theological connection between what is expected of them as preacher, pastor, and leader of a community of worship, on the one hand, and as a leader of relevant ethical and social change on the other. The ecumenical theology as developed in the United States by Reinhold Niebuhr gave a possible basis for such a unity in a pastor's task. And those who truly base their ministry on such a theology, whether in center city or suburbia, find the pastorate exciting, challenging, and of infinite worth. Those who have lost an appreciation of what a worshiping community may be become frustrated social workers or politicians. And those who give up on the radical ethical drive of the gospel break under the pressures and irrelevancies of trying to be a professional chaplain to an essentially secular people.

Five rather intense external pressures are at work on the Church, the response to which will determine in large part what the Church will be in 1975. I have space but to mention them.

War as the instrument of national policy. Since Hitler almost singlehandedly liquidated the decisive influence of the pacifist movement in U.S. churches, they have really had nothing important to say to the nation in the area of war and peace. The churches on the whole did better during World War II than during World War I. At least most pastors avoided the complete betrayal of the gospel in their restrained support of the war effort. Dr. Niebuhr's sophisticated ethics helped many to avoid ethical romanticism on the one hand and ethical capitulation on the other.

Aside from a growing support of the United Nations, the Church has had little to stand for in this area of increasing concern in the last twenty years. It has refused to be pacifist, although supporting the rights of conscientious objectors to war; and it was too sophisticated to support United World Federalists. But most of what it said has sounded like analyses of foreign policy by third-echelon State Department people who are not responsible for actual policy.

The greatest threat to the Church in the immediate future is that it will fail to have anything to say against those who urge our Government to use our nuclear power to keep us safe. Since local congregations still have great difficulty in transcending the values and interests of their immediate communities, the question is whether the sense of world community can influence them away from unthinking and unqualified support of our national policy, whatever it becomes. Late last year Cardinal Spellman quoted Stephen Decatur ("My country right or wrong . . .") with approval and Daniel Poling wrote to *The New York Times* implying that the National Council of Churches' statement on Vietnam was unpatriotic.

Race as the new divisive issue. Since the late forties, the popular mind has taken it for granted that the tension between communism and the free world is the chief menace to peace and order. Now race threatens to become the key issue both nationally and internationally. Since June, 1963, the churches have been attempting to play a decisive role here. They contributed much to the establishment of an enlightened U.S. political position, in contrast to the policy of South Africa or Rhodesia.

But unless the churches can move forward to the actual and voluntary establishment of a new pluralistic nondiscriminatory pattern of race relations here and abroad, they will have failed at a crucial moment of history. Conversion to color blindness is the number one challenge to Christian evangelism. Any other evangelism is a betrayal of the gospel.

Poverty as the new challenge. In the old days when individuals by their enterprise and energy could easily break the shackles of poverty in this country, it was not so fatal that the Church had given up biblical economics in favor of bourgeois capitalism. The American churches have barely begun to realize that an issue fully as divisive as race must be attacked and quickly. Poverty at home and abroad challenges the Church to do more basic social thinking than has occurred since the Federal Council of Churches was established half a century ago and came out on the side of the workingman and his unions.

Urbanization and cybernetics. It was Malthus who scared our fathers with the specter of geometric population growth. We had better begin to be frightened again. Technology of production and distribution promises to keep pace with the population growth despite Malthus' fears. But the problem of the city (which no religion has ever really handled well) and the problem of which programs will be fed into the governing computers can well give any Christian nightmares. Since there is no indication that anyone in political power really takes the gospel very seriously, it is likely that the churches will not directly affect what is being decided for the people of the next decades. They will do well if they are able to defend themselves and their own freedom to be free and human.

Secularistic relativism. One must have a certain sympathy with those conservative Christians who attack contextual ethics these days. Considerable ethical sophistication is required to make the distinction between contextual ethics and the growing secularistic relativism in morals.

The Church has always found it difficult to produce saints who could at the same time transcend a too rigid conception of moral law and not succumb to the temptations of the world. It is not yet clear whether the new freedom set forth in the most popular treatments of Christian ethics these days will produce men responsible enough under God to be distinguished from modern men of and in the world, who appear to believe that personal morality is entirely relative. In the next period the Church will be hard pressed by the secular relativist in ethics and must stimulate its members to the kind of moral conviction that a pragmatic America so greatly needs.

In the light of these pressures, both internal and external, I suggest the following priorities for the next decade.

The Church must identify itself much more radically with the interests of the poor, the "losers," the outcasts, and the alienated. While one of the American Church's great strengths is its direct channel to the power structure of the nation through its most influential members, it will be disastrous if the Church pulls back from the course tentatively begun (e.g., civil rights activism and involvement in community action programs in the cities) in order to preserve undiminished this influence on the power structure. The mark of the presence of the awaited Messiah is still related to the poor having the gospel preached to them and the captives being released. The American Church would be foolish to ignore suburbia and the concerns of influential members, but its life will depend on involving many of these members in the social revolution that will continue to develop in the cities of this nation.

In addition to the parish congregations that still remain the essential form and substance, the Church must further develop specialized ministries in the cities, colleges and universities, and in labor unions and industries. So far most of the "pilot projects" have not led the way to program patterns that are repeatable. When the charismatic leader is called away, too many specialized ministries promptly fold up or are domesticated by buildings and budgets.

I do not agree with those who have given up on the parish congregation. But I am sure that to the extent that twentieth-century city life is our concern, the Church dare not center all its life and money inside the great stone piles that still dot the urban scene. The people, especially the poor and the powerful, are just not there. New patterns of involvement in mission and service at both ends of the social spectrum must be developed.

The denominations must further develop unity in mission and service. In 1946 I addressed the plenary meeting of the Federal Council of Churches in Seattle on the subject "The Evangelization of America." I do not remember much of what I said, except that I made the point that unless the denominations radically changed their expenditures from separate sectarian programs toward united ecumenical programs, no one could take seriously their claim to be interested in the evangelization of America. Twenty years later I stand by that statement.

I would add, however, one additional conviction that arises out of the last fifteen years of national ecumenical involvement. Although budget appropriation still gives a useful index to the seriousness of the denominations' ecumenical concern, I am more impressed today than I was in 1946 by the need for the national denominational leadership to give their time to developing united programs. The most excellent interdenominational staff that can be recruited cannot do the job without the major involvement of the churches' leadership in planning programs and implementing them.

And to any who have given up on councils of churches because of their frustrations with them, I would say that the only alternative is to proceed at once toward church union. Sectarian mission is not a viable alternative in 1966.

Increasing involvement of lay men and women must be a prime objective of the Church. Such involvement means a revolution in the thinking of most ministers and lay people. Presently few ministers are able to speak effectively to their members or to hear their members speaking to them. The theological insight of most ministers is entirely inadequate, and that of most lay people is nonexistent.

The best channel for the world to speak to the Church is through the lay members engrossed in that world. The best channel for the gospel to reach the world is from theologians through ministers through lay members. The channel presently seems blocked both ways.

Finally, the Church must get on with her theological work. Although I began this article with the observation that the ecumenical theology that has most affected our churches and all of us for the last half-century is under increasing criticism, I confess that I do not see anything better on the horizon. Perhaps Dietrich

Bonhoeffer could have provided it had he not been martyred. Maybe William Temple would have had even more to contribute if he had lived ten years longer.

Whatever the reason, no strong theological voice is yet heard to redirect the Church on its pilgrim way for this next decade. We must pray for such a new and persuasive voice. For always it is more important that theological assumptions be examined and corrected than that conclusions or programs be disputed.